INVESTING IN STOCKS

Maximize your profit and make money with this guide for beginners and advanced traders. Learn stock trading strategies, secrets, techniques and crash the Bear Market

MARK KRATTER

Table of Contents

Introduction

When you learned to drive, you didn't just jump in the car and turn it on. Instead, someone walked you through exactly what to do before you started the car. You were told what the stick-shift or automatic PRNDL (Park-Reverse-Neutral-Drive-Low) was for. You were told how to move the mirrors, what was forward and reverse, and other buttons in the car. Before you invest in the stock market, you need to walk, not run. You need a guide that tells you how things work, so you avoid making costly mistakes. As long as you know how something works, you don't have to be afraid of the reality of it. Many people do not understand investing, so the stock market scares them. The reality is—you just need to know how it works, the parts that make it work, and you can set up an investment strategy that works.

A stock is usually referred to as a share. It is a share in a company that is looking for investors. These investors provide capital for the company to grow the company. When a company first offers shares, it is called an IPO or Initial Public Offering. The share price is set on the estimated worth of the company, as well as the number of shares available for sale.

For the shares to be publicly offered, a company needs to be listed on a stock exchange, like the NYSE (New York Stock Exchange). Traders and investors can then buy and sell stocks, but the company will only make money with the IPO. After the IPO is over, it is simply businessmen, individuals, and investors trading the stocks between themselves to make a profit and dividends.

Buying Shares on the Stock Market

Investors and traders sell stocks after the IPO based on the perceived value. A company's value can go up or down, which is where investors make their money. A company's stock price that rises can provide a profit. If an investor has purchased those shares and the price or company value decreases, then the investor will lose money. It is also the investors and traders that will push the price in an up or down direction.

Investors have one of two goals: investing in the short or the long term. A long-term investment is based on a stock continuing to rise in price. A short-term investment is to gain quick cash and pulling out before the stock price decreases.

Mature companies offer dividends to their shareholders. If you have stocks, then you are a shareholder in a company. If you hold the stocks long enough and have enough stock in a company, you can vote on new board members. Dividends are company profits that you get a cut of.

Investors will make money on the price fluctuations and dividends. A seller is often trying to gain a profit by selling to a new buyer. The new buyer is also trying to buy-in as low as possible, so that when the stock price continues to increase, they will make a profit.

The profit is calculated by taking the initial buy-in price and subtracting it from the closing or sale price. For example, if you buy into Google at $400 and wait for it to go up to $600, then the profit is $200 per share.

Sellers can push the price down due to supply and demand. This financial market works based on supply and demand.

Supply and Demand Concept

You should already know that in economics, when there is an oversupply of a product, the price is low. There is no demand for the product; therefore, a company or, in this case, a stock is not of interest.

When there is an undersupply of something like a stock, the demand is high. With more interested parties, a price will continue to increase.

If there is an even amount of supply and demand, then equality exists, and there is no movement to see.

For the stock market, when too many people sell a stock, the price will decline. When too many people buy a stock, the price will continue to rise. If there is an equal number of shares and interests, then the price usually trades sideways because there is a balance.

As you learn about the stock market, you will hear the word volume, often. Volume is the number of shares that change hands on a daily basis. Millions of shares can be traded on the stock exchange in a day as investors attempt to make money from increasing or decreasing prices.

The stock market works based on the interest or volume of traders. If a stock does not have any volume or very little, then it is not being actively traded; thus the price is not moving. Traders such as market makers get into the market in order to buy or sell stocks for companies with low volume. They do not stop a stock from rising or falling. Instead, market makers just try to garner interest in the company's stock.

What Most People Do

When it comes to the stock market and traders, most individuals are looking for the high-volume trades, with fluctuating prices. They get in, make a profit, and get out to find the next big profit.

Final Thoughts

The shares are first released from a company to gain investment funds. The shares are then traded as a way to garner dividends and profit from the up and downtrends in the market. The market also allows you to invest in various exchanges around the world, as long as your broker provides access. Most people trade in their country's stock market or the largest in their region like the Japan Stock Exchange, London Stock Exchange, and NYSE.

CHAPTER 1:

Information About the Stock Market

A stock is a form of security that suggests proportional ownership in a company. Stocks are acquired and sold predominantly on stock exchanges; however, there can be private arrangements as well. These exchanges/trades need to fit within government laws, which are expected to shield investors from misleading practices. Stocks can be obtained from a large number of online platforms.

Businesses issue (offer) stock to raise capital. The holder of stock (a shareholder) has now acquired a portion of the company and shares its profit and loss. Therefore, a shareholder is considered an owner of the company. Ownership is constrained by the amount of shares an individual owns in regard to the amount of shares the company is divided into. For example, if a company has 1,000 shares of stock, and one individual owns 100 shares, that individual would receive 10% of the company's capital and profits.

Financial experts don't own companies as such; instead, they sell shares offered by companies. Under the law, there are different types of companies, and some are viewed as independent because of how they have set up their businesses. Regardless of the type of company, ultimately, they must report costs, income, changes in structure, etc., or they can be sued. A business set up as an "independent," known as a sole proprietorship, suggests that the owner assumes all responsibilities and is liable for all financial aspects of the business. A business set up as a company of any sort means that the business is separate from its owners, and the owners aren't personally responsible for the financial aspects of the business.

This separation is of extreme importance; it limits the commitment of both the company and the shareholder/owner.

If the business comes up short, a judge may rule for the company to be liquidated–however, your very own assets will not come under threat. The court can't demand that you sell your shares, though the value of your shares will have fallen significantly.

What Is Trading?

Trading is the basic idea of exchanging one thing for another. In this regard, it is buying or selling, where compensation is paid by a buyer to a seller. Trade can happen inside an economy among sellers and buyers. Overall, trade allows countries to develop markets for the exchange of goods and services that, for the most part, wouldn't have been available otherwise. It is the reason why an American purchaser can choose between a Japanese, German, or American conduit. Due to overall trade, the market contains progressively significant competition, which makes it possible for buyers to get products and services at affordable costs.

In fiscal markets, trading implies the buying and selling of insurances; for instance, the purchase of stock on the New York Stock Exchange (NYSE).

Fundamentals of Stock/Securities Exchange

The exchange of stocks and securities happen on platforms like the New York Stock Exchange and Nasdaq. Stocks are recorded on a specific exchange, which links buyers and sellers, allowing them to trade those stocks. The trade is tracked in the market and allows buyers to get company stocks at fair prices. The value of these stocks moves – up or down – depending on many factors in the market. Investors are able to look at these factors and make a decision on whether or not they want to purchase these stocks.

A market record tracks the value of a stock, which either addresses the market with everything taken into account or specific fragments of the market. You're likely going to hear most about the S&P 500, the Nasdaq composite and the Dow Jones Industrial Average in this regard.

Financial advisors use data to benchmark the value of their own portfolios and, some of the time, to shed light on their stock exchanging decisions. You can also put your assets into an entire portfolio based on the data available in the market.

Stock Exchanging Information

Most financial experts would be well-taught to build a portfolio with a variety of different financial assets. However, experts who prefer a greater degree of movement take more interest in the stock exchange. This type of investment incorporates the buying and selling of stocks.

The goal of people who trade in stock is to use market data and things happening in the market to either sell stocks for a profit or buy stocks at low prices to make a profit later. Some stock traders are occasional investors, which means they buy and sell every now and then. Others are serious investors, making as little as twelve exchanges for every month.

Financial experts who exchange stocks do wide research, as often as possible, devoting hours day by day tracking the market. They rely upon particular audits, using instruments to chart a stock's advancements attempting to find trading openings and examples. Various online mediators offer stock exchanging information, including expert reports, stock research, and charting tools.

What Is A Bear Market?

A bear market means stock prices are falling—limits move to 20% or more. Progressive financial experts may be alright with the term bear market. Profiting in the trade business will always far outlast the typical bear market, which is why in a bear market, smart investors will hold their shares until the market recovers. This has been seen time and time again.

The S&P 500, which holds around 500 of the greatest stocks in the U.S., has consistently maintained an average of around 7% consistently when you factor in reinvested profits and varied growth. That suggests that if you invested $1,000 30 years ago, you could have around $7,600 today.

Stock market crash versus a correction

A crash happens when the commercial value prices fall by 10% or more. It is an unexpected, incredibly sharp fall in stock prices; for example, in October 1987, when stocks dove 23% in a single day.

The stock market tends to be affected longer by crashes in the market and can last from two to nine years.

The criticalness of improvement

You can't avoid the possibility of bear markets or the economy crashing, or even losing money while trading. What you can do, however, is limit the effects these types of markets will have on your investment by maintaining a diversified portfolio.

Diversification shields your portfolio from unavoidable market risks.

If you dump a large portion of your cash into one means of investment, you're betting on growth that can rapidly turn to loss by a large number of factors.

To cushion risks, financial specialists expand by pooling different types of stocks together, offsetting the inevitable possibility that one stock will crash and your entire portfolio will be affected or you lose everything.

You can put together individual stocks and assets in a single portfolio. One recommendation: dedicate 10% or less of your portfolio to a few stocks you believe in each time you decide to invest.

Ways to Invest

There are different ways for new investors to purchase stocks. If you need to pay very low fees, you will need to invest additional time making your own trades. If you wish to beat the market, however, you'll pay higher charges by getting someone to trade on your behalf. If you don't have the time or interest, you may need to make do with lower results.

Most stock purchasers get anxious when the market is doing well. Incredibly, this makes them purchase stocks when they are the most volatile. Obviously, business share that is not performing well triggers fear. That makes most investors sell when the costs are low.

The Comportment of the Stock Market

The stock market, like other businesses, has its ups and downs depending on the operations of how investors alter their financial prices concerning the market equilibrium.

Prices of stocks typically shift and may affect the stock market either positively or negatively. When talking about the market equilibrium, investors may become optimists, therefore driving prices to become quite high benefiting traders. Similarly, they may become pessimists, eventually driving prices too low, resulting in losses and a decline of stock value. This has led economists to debate and determine if stock markets are essential and useful.

According to the interpretation of different economists, there are multiple factors that contribute to these trends in the stock market. Some of the common elements have been linked to political and financial news originating from different sources. Irrationality in the market is another aspect but also depends significantly on economic news and other relevant market events. Crashes in the stock market are mostly a negative outcome when the stock market value deteriorates, leading to the loss of billions in companies and among investors.

Crashes are primarily attributed to panics, and loss of confidence with the most known crashes include the Wall Street Crash of 1929, Stock Market Crash of 2008, and Black Monday of 1987.

Over the years and the crashes witnessed before, different market analysts have come up with means of predicting how the stock market operates. Using trading strategies, the technique identifies online precursors based on Google trends searched data regarding shares. When the search volume is too high, it hence suggests that there are possibilities of losses in the future. Similarly, the decline in search volumes indicates that the stock market will become stable in the coming few months. The prices of stocks usually captured in the form of stock market indices, therefore, vary depending on the search data volume. Some of the indexes include the FTSE, Euronext, and S&P.

CHAPTER 2:

Understanding the Basics of Investing in Stocks

Before getting into stock trading, you have to realize how to pick the correct stocks, which requires a top to bottom comprehension of an organization's yearly report and financial proclamations. Figure out how to comprehend what stock truly speaks to in an organization, and how to decide the genuine value of any stock.

This enables you to settle on better-investing choices by staying away from the expensive mix-up of obtaining an organization's stock when the market has pushed its offer cost excessively high with respect to its value.

Financial Terms

All through the accompanying data, you'll run over financial terms with which you may not yet be recognizable. Without going into extraordinary profundity, you'll see the accompanying terms ordinarily utilized:

- **Income per Share:** The all-out organization benefit isolated by the quantity of stock offers exceptional.

- **Opening up to the world:** Slang for when an organization intends to have an IPO of its stock.

- **Initial public offering**: Short for Initial Public Offering; when an organization sells its portions of stock just because.

- **Market Cap:** Short for Market Capitalization. The measure of cash you would need to pay in the event that you purchased each and every portion of stock in an organization (to compute market top, duplicate the quantity of offers by the value per share).

- **Offer:** An offer, or a solitary regular stock, speaks to one unit of a financial specialist's possession in a portion of the benefits, misfortunes, and resources of an organization. An organization makes shares when it cuts itself into pieces and offers them to speculators in return for money.

- **Ticker Symbol:** A short gathering of letters that speaks to a specific stock as recorded on the stock market. For instance, The Coca-Cola Company has a ticker image of KO, and Johnson and Johnson have a ticker image of JNJ.

- **Financier:** The financial foundation or investment bank that does the majority of the administrative work and organizes an organization's IPO.

Growing a Business with Equity

When figuring out how to value an organization, it comprehends the idea of a business and the stock market. Pretty much every huge enterprise began as a little, mother and-pop activity, and through development, wound up financial mammoths.

Consider Walmart, Amazon, and McDonald's. Walmart was initially a solitary store business in Arkansas. Amazon started as an online book retailer in a carport. McDonald's was before a little eatery that nobody outside of San Bernardino, California had ever heard of. How did these little organizations develop from modest, main residence ventures to three of the biggest organizations in the American economy? They raised capital by selling stock in themselves.

As an organization develops, it keeps on confronting the obstacle of collecting enough cash to finance continuous extension. Proprietors, for the most part, have two alternatives to beat this. They can either acquire the cash from a bank or financial speculator or offer a piece of the business to speculators and utilize the cash to subsidize development. Organizations regularly take out a bank credit, since it's ordinarily simple to procure, and valuable, to a limited extent.

Banks won't generally loan cash to organizations, and over-anxious administrators may attempt to get excessively, which adds a great deal of obligation to the organization's monetary record and damages its exhibition measurements. Factors, for example, these frequently incite littler, developing organizations to issue stock. In return for surrendering a little division of possession control, they get money to extend the business.

Notwithstanding cash that doesn't need to be paid back, opening up to the world, as it's considered when an organization sells stock in itself just because, gives the business chiefs and proprietors another device. Rather than paying money for specific exchanges, for example, an obtaining of another organization or business line, they can utilize their own stock.

How Is Stock Issued?

To all the more likely see how issuing stock functions, take the anecdotal organization "ABC Furniture, Inc." After getting hitched, a youthful couple chose to begin a business. This enables them to work for themselves, just as orchestrate their working hours around their family. Both a couple have consistently had a solid enthusiasm for furniture, so they choose to open a store in the place where they grew up.

In the wake of acquiring cash from the bank, they name their organization "ABC Furniture" and start a new business. During the initial couple of years, the organization makes little benefit since they put the profit over into the store, purchasing extra stock, redesigning, and extending the structure to oblige the expanding level of product.

After ten years, the business has developed quickly. The couple has figured out how to satisfy the organization's obligation and have benefits of more than $500,000 every year. Persuaded that ABC Furniture could also do in a few bigger neighboring urban areas, the couple chooses they need to open two new branches.

They look into their alternatives and discover that they need over $4 million to grow. Not having any desire to acquire cash and need to make obligation and premium installments once more, they choose to fund-raise by offering value to potential investors, so they sell stock in their organization.

The organization approaches a guarantor for the stock offering, for example, Goldman Sachs or JP Morgan, who dives into their financial proclamations and decides the value of the business. As referenced, ABC Furniture wins $500,000 after-charge benefits every year. It additionally has a book value of $3 million, which means the value of the land, building, stock, and different resources, in the wake of covering the organization's obligation. The guarantor inquiries about and finds the normal furniture stock exchanges available at multiple times its organization's profit.

I'm not catching this' meaning. Just expressed, you would duplicate the organization's income of $500,000 by 20. For ABC's situation, this outcome in a market value estimation of $10 million. In the event that you include the organization's book value, and you land at

$13 million. This implies, in the financier's assessment, that ABC Furniture has an all-out value of $13 million.

An Example

The youthful couple, presently in their 30's, must choose the amount of the organization they are eager to sell. At the present time, they claim 100% of the business. The more organization shares they sell, the more money they'll raise, yet they should remember that by selling more, they'll be surrendering a bigger piece of their proprietorship. As the organization develops, that proprietorship will be worth more, so an insightful businessperson would not sell more than the person needed to.

Subsequent to talking about it, the couple chooses to stay with 60% of the offer and the other 40% to general society as stock. When you crunch the numbers, this implies they will keep $7.8 million worth of the business, and in light of the fact that they possess a larger part of the stock, more noteworthy than 50%, they will at present be responsible for the store.

The other 40% of the stock that they offered to the open has a value of $5.2 million. The guarantor discovers financial specialists who need to purchase the stock and gives a check for $5.2 million to the couple.

In spite of the fact that they possess less of the organization, the proprietors' stake will ideally develop quicker since they have the way to extend quickly. Utilizing the cash from their open offering, ABC

Furniture effectively opens the two new stores and has $1.2 million in real money left finished, since they raised $5.2 million yet just utilized $4 million.

Their business performs far and away superior in the new branches. The two new stores make around $800,000 every year in benefit each, while the old store still makes the equivalent $500,000. Between the three stores, ABC presently makes a yearly benefit of $2.1 million.

In spite of the fact that they don't have the adaptability of a private company or the opportunity to just close shop any longer, their organization is currently valued at $51 million. You would arrive at this by increasing their net income of $2.1 million every year by 20 (the normal furniture stock various referenced before) and include the organization's most recent book value of $9 million since each store has a book value of $3 million. The couple's 60% stake currently has an absolute worth of $30.6 million.

With this model, it's anything but difficult to perceive how independent ventures appear to detonate in value when they open up to the world. The first proprietors of the organization, one might say, become wealthier medium-term. The sum they could remove from the business was restricted to the benefit that was created. Presently, the proprietors can sell their offers in the organization whenever, raising money rapidly.

This procedure frames the premise of Wall Street. The stock market works as a huge closeout where proprietorship in organizations like ABC Furniture are offered to the most elevated bidder every day. As a result of human instinct and the feelings of dread and covetousness, an organization can sell for unmistakably more than or for far not as much as its characteristic value. A decent financial specialist figures out how to distinguish those organizations as of now selling underneath their actual worth with the goal that they can purchase whatever number offers as could be allowed.

CHAPTER 3:

Types of Stocks

Choosing stocks isn't difficult, but it is complicated. What that means is that all of the steps are simple, but there are a lot of them. The first things you need to understand are what different kinds of stocks there are, what they do, and what they can do for you. Since a good portfolio must be diverse, you can think of each type of stock as a different kind of building block. Which blocks you choose to include will depend on what shape you want the finished structure to take.

Types of Stocks:

1. Common Stocks

It's an equity product, meaning it gives you ownership of the profits in an entity. Each share is equal to one voter's stake in the election of the board, which you'll remember makes the decisions for how the profit and shares should be used. They are a high risk/high reward investment because there is no protection from the fluctuations of the market, but also there is no middleman between the stockholder and the share of the profits that they own. If the company goes under, the shareholder is the last to be paid, coming after debtors, bondholders and the owners of preferred stock. This last category brings us to our next one.

2. Preferred Stocks

An easy way to think of preferred stocks is as lying between a debt and equity. Normally a preferred stock will guarantee dividends to be paid each year indefinitely. Obviously, if a company has to liquidate, these dividends will stop, but the preferred stockholder will be paid back the current price of the shares before a common stockholder. Additionally, preferred stocks often do not come with a vote in the company decisions the way common stocks do. Because the dividends are fixed, this type of stock is a good choice for corporate portfolios where they balance risk.

3. Growth Stocks

These are stocks whose historical record indicates that they are growing and will grow faster than the economy now and in the near future. Obviously, this is subject to a lot of change and variation. What is a growth stock today that could stagnate next week, depending on the health of the company and multiple other factors? Brokers are always keeping an eye out for these stocks, so they tend to be priced at the highest point the market will bear. Their risk assessment is usually in the average to higher-than-average range.

4. Blue Chip (or Bellwether) Stocks

Blue Chip stocks are the reliable bets of the stock market. These are stocks that are usually old companies that have been performing steadily, paying off respectable dividends for years or even decades. Their risk profile is low to moderately low, and brokers tend to hold them long-term.

5. Income Stocks

The main point of differentiation between these and other stocks is the number of dividends that are paid out each quarter. This is where they get their name; 50-80% is typically sent to the stockholder regularly, and that acts just like any other income. These shares are typically in companies that are older, mature, and moderately paced growers. The risk is low to moderately low because they aren't expected to rise drastically in the share price. That might sound bad, but it isn't the point of owning these stocks, the dividend is.

6. Value Stocks

A somewhat subjective term, a "value stock" is one that is considered underpriced in relation to its potential. This potential is determined by looking at the company's earnings and other measures that we'll tackle when talking about how to choose a stock. Once you have those skills down, you'll be proficient at finding stocks that are a good value for money.

7. Cyclical Stocks

When share prices historically track with the economy overall, we refer to them as "cyclical." This means that when times are booming, these companies boom along with them, and when times are tougher, their fortunes tend to fall as well. Companies in industries like airlines, automobiles, and construction tend to fall into this category. The important thing to recognize about this type of stock is that in the short term, their risk level is relatively high, but because they almost always rebound, that risk is lowered significantly when held over a long period of time.

8. Defensive Stocks

Companies that fall in this category can be thought of as the opposite of Cyclical Stocks. They are less vulnerable to economic shake-ups because they're in industries that people buy from in any economic climate. Things like utilities, food, and drug companies are in this category. They are on the lower end of the risk spectrum, and usually modest but steady earners. This can change though, depending on new products and other factors, so don't discount them in a risk-tolerant portfolio.

9. Speculative Stocks

These are stocks that do not have a strong recent earnings history but for other reasons show promise. Some dot-com startups fall into this category as do established companies that have taken a downturn but are under new and exciting management or introducing a promising product. These are very high-risk investments, but the reward can be enormous.

10. Share Class

Typically, each share comes with a percentage of ownership in the company and one vote in the control of the company (usually for the board of directors who make decisions about the way stock is used). In some cases, a company will split the stock into two classes, and one will carry more voting weight. This allows the company to ensure that a small number of people make the decisions. It also prevents an outside investor from being able to buy up enough stock to affect a hostile takeover. In a company like this, the shares would be labeled Class A and Class B and displayed with their company name on the ticker with a lowercase letter that signifies this. For example, if the company's abbreviation was ABC the ticker would read ABCa and ABCb.

Class B stocks are usually the common stock of the company, with each share entitling the owner to one vote. Class A stocks still represent the same percentage of the company in terms of ownership but would confer say, 10 votes per share.

The final key difference is that if the company goes bankrupt and its assets must be liquidated, Class A shareholders will be paid before Class B shareholders. Note: all debts must first be repaid before any of the shareholders are paid.

CHAPTER 4:

Types of Brokers

When you want to invest in the stock market, you should choose the right broker. This is the only way you can invest in the market if you are a beginner. Brokers will help you make the right decisions about how to invest in stocks. A broker does not have to advise you but will perform other functions.

Regular Brokers

Regular brokers are those people whose job is only to buy or sell stocks or shares for you. This is the job requirement, but they will not suggest which stocks you should invest in. Some part-time brokers will only invest in those shares that you tell them to invest in. When you hire these brokers, you can start by investing in the market on the right foot. Since regular brokers are not always tied to firms, you can hire independent brokers too. These brokers will charge you for their services, and some of these brokers will mislead people into investing in those stocks that will benefit them or other people. You should always perform the right research and due diligence to understand which stock you should invest in.

Full-Time Brokers

As mentioned earlier, full-time brokers are those who are hired to take care of an investor's portfolio. These brokers are specialized and have good knowledge of the stock market. They perform the right analysis to understand the stocks better, so they can help investors make profits. Since these brokers know which stock to invest in, they will tell you which stock you should invest in. You will need to spend a little more when you choose to invest in a full-time broker since they spend all their time helping you out. If you are new to investing in the market, you can hire a full-time broker to help you with investing in it. These brokers will buy the stocks and sell them based on your risk tolerance. Most full-time brokers are not interested in investing in stocks since the trend is hard to predict. Full-time brokers prefer to invest in large companies since the price of these stocks is predictable. Therefore, choose a full-time broker if you want to invest only in stocks.

Boiler Room Brokers

Boiler room brokers are those people who are only around to mislead the public. These brokers are people you should avoid engaging with. They identify those traders who do not know their stuff and cheat them. These people know all the tricks of the trade and know-how to influence any stock in the market. When they influence the price of the stock, they can either increase or decrease the demand for that stock. You should be wary of a boiler room broker, and it is hard for you to find one. These brokers will act like they are interested in giving you the right information, but that is not what they want to do.

Online Traders

Online traders are those people who look at stocks on the Internet. When you hire an online trader, they will invest your funds in stocks in the market based on the online analysis that they perform. An online trader can either work independently or in a firm. These traders study the market and can give you advice about the market. Online traders prefer that you only trade in predictable stocks. It is easier to understand the risk of such stocks. These traders will charge you more than regular brokers since they have a lot of experience. If you are starting with trading now and want to learn how to invest in stocks, you should choose an online broker. You must ensure that you differentiate between honest and fraudulent brokers.

Floor Brokers

Floor brokers are people who can operate in the stock market only from the floor or the base of the stock exchange. These brokers cannot make their decisions but will follow the orders given to them by their brokers or investors. You cannot find the right floor broker to help you with investing. It is a good idea to avoid choosing floor brokers to help you invest since they do not give you the right advice. So, you should avoid looking for a floor broker. You should look at the different types of brokers and see the type of broker that will suit your needs or requirements best. They will help you invest in the right stocks.

CHAPTER 5:

Factors to Consider When Hiring a Stock Broker

You will definitely end up with more than one stockbroker that you have to compare. At the end of your comparison, you should hire just one, who will provide all the services and help that you will need as you get started in stock trading. Below are some factors that will make choosing the right one easy:

i)   The cost

Stock brokers differ in the way that they charge for their services. If he is offering the kinds of services that you are looking for, and he is a well reputable broker, you will go to the one that charges the least amount of money so as to maximize the returns that you get out of your investment. Some stockbrokers charge commissions plus other charges, so you have to consider all these charges before settling to one stockbroker.

ii)   Stockbroker capabilities

Expert stockbrokers can advise you on the right kinds of investments to go for so as to ensure that you are not losing any money in the end. If you want a stockbroker that will be responsible for buying and selling your stocks, it is best to go for the most capable because he will always make the right decisions for your gain. Check out the past record of the stockbroker, and you will be able to choose the best one to deal with.

iii)   Trust

This is very important since the stockbroker will be managing your account and all the money that your stocks will be generating. Licensed stockbrokers can be trusted. You can also get a referral from someone that is currently using a trustworthy stockbroker so as to be at ease even as you trust him with your investments. It is always good to conduct a background check on the stockbroker you are interested in so that you will be sure that he is trustworthy and quite reputable.

iv)   The company or firm he represents

Many stockbrokers work for a certain brokerage company and so, you have to check out more about this company before you can hire their services. Ensure that the company is reputable, with a good track record of performance and very capable to manage your investments. So many people are investing in stocks these days so it, will be so easy to get the information you need about a certain brokerage company or firm.

v)   The kinds of services they offer

When hiring any kinds of services, it is always good to determine how the service provider serves his clients. Choose a stock broker that will give you quality support services every time that you need them. Some stockbrokers are known to treat their clients unprofessionally, or to be unavailable at odd hours, which is not something you would go for. Ensure that they have the best customer support services so that you will always be treated as a valuable customer.

Types of Stock Broker Fees

Both the full-service and discount stockbrokers charge a certain fee for their services to their clients as stated here:

a) Commissions: This is the fee charged by the stockbroker who executes your buying and selling of stocks. This fee is charged per transaction that the stockbroker executes. Discount stockbrokers charge a relatively lower commission when compared to a full-service stockbroker. Always compare the commissions charged by different stock brokers before you can proceed to work with them to be sure that you are not paying more money than you should.

b) Asset-based management fees: Stock brokers will charge you a certain percentage of your total assets that are under their management instead of charging commissions of the same. Their annual fees do not usually go beyond 2%, so it is usually not a huge amount of money, although this depends on the stockbroker you are dealing with.

c) Premier account: Premier accounts are offered by stockbrokers to the investors that want to enjoy more services from their stock investment accounts. If you upgrade to this kind of account, you will be charged an amount of money, but you will be able to enjoy credit cards, checking accounts and other great services depending on the stockbroker that you are dealing with.

d) IRA custodial fees: You will be charged for any IRA related paperwork that your stockbroker will do for you. Even though some stockbrokers' waiver such fees, they end up charging their clients on a yearly basis.

e) Inactivity fees: This is the fees charged for those investors that have been unable to generate a certain amount of fees or commissions as per their agreement with the stockbroker. This means that you have to be active throughout to avoid paying this fee.

Trading in Stocks without the Help of Stockbrokers

The role of a stockbroker is very paramount when it comes to stock investing. Stockbrokers are supposed to make work easier for investors, and the stock market is designed in such a manner that it can be really hard for an investor to do it himself, although this does not mean that it is impossible. If, for instance, you are the kind of investor that does not trade frequently, you may want to save some money and decide to sell your stocks directly without the help of a stockbroker.

Selling your stocks directly will involve a much longer process, and this means that it will take more time than if a stockbroker was helping you with the sale. Another thing to note is that you will not have control over the stock price. This means that you could sell your stocks at a much lower price than you could have anticipated.

These days, investment firms allow investors to trade in their stocks directly without necessarily involving a stockbroker. The role of a stockbroker in the modern-day stock market is slowly diminishing as many people look for ways to minimize the expenses and maximize the returns.

Different ways to do this are:

- Contact the transfer agent of the company whose shares you want to sell and see if he can be of help to you. If he agrees, you will send your shares directly to him. In this case, you will be required to sign the stock certificates and hand them over to him, and then you will agree on the cost of the stocks, and the deal will be sealed. Some transfer agents will charge a small fee for this, but most of them offer such services for free, so if you are lucky, you will not be charged a dime. The recent average share price will be used to determine the cost of the stocks that you are selling.

- Direct purchase plans will not require you to have a stockbroker as well. Many corporations usually buy and sell their shares through direct purchase plans or through dividend reinvestment, and this is a sure way to trade in stocks on your own. The plan will always keep your stocks in the account, and it allows reinvestments of your dividends in order to increase the number of shares you own in that company. If you want to sell your shares, you can contact the plan administrator for an easier trading. The cost of stocks, in this case, will be determined by the recent average share price.

- You are allowed to sell your shares directly to your friends or relatives without necessarily involving a stockbroker. What you need for this transaction are your stock certificates. The buyer will only need to have money or a certified check. Just endorse the shares to the buyer and sign on them. You may want to check out other requirements that the company's transfer agent will need so that you will seal the deal without wasting so much time on it.

- Set up an online brokerage account and take full control of your buying and selling of stocks. The internet has brought so many changes in the stock market, and this is just one of them. What you need to find on the internet is an online trading company. These days, there are so many online trading companies that will allow you to set up an account and start trading in stocks. If you have studied stock investing in detail and you are sure that you can do it, this is the way to go so you will not have to deal with a stockbroker ever again.

If, on the other hand, you are a frequent trader in the stock market and you would want to invest more money in more stocks, it is always good to have a stockbroker as his services could come in handy when you need any kind of help with your investments.

CHAPTER 6:

Fundamental Analysis

The Fundamental Analysis is a particular type of financial market analysis that seeks to identify the price of an instrument being studied, starting from the main causes that can move the prices of an index, currency pair, shares or any other financial instrument.

The goal is always to get a profit from your trading operations, so if for example we consider the price of a stock we will find those characteristics for which the stock should be appreciated or depreciated, therefore we position ourselves in the direction of the market which is considered right based on the analysis. All this by resorting to the study of balance sheet data, economic dynamics, the evolution of interest rates or the balance of payments, etc. In short, after a careful analysis of fundamental type is tipped to buy a financial instrument when the current price is less than the theoretical, to obtain in this way a capital gain (profit).

It's actually very difficult to use the factors cited to predict the future trend of prices; in fact, often, this type of analysis is time-consuming and specific technical skills. Time and skills that are necessary to verify and analyze data that can be extrapolated from various information channels. However, this approach assumes that the market is rational and efficient, but the market is not always like this. Whenever you open the trading platform to trade, you must never forget that behind the numbers and the sophisticated graphics of a program, there are always the people who are the real players in the market. And people, as emotional beings, are always and constantly in the grip of their emotions.

Today, technology has really made great strides, there is artificial intelligence and robots of all kinds, and also in the trading sector, and we have something that looks a lot like robots. I'm talking about automatic trading systems, the so-called trading system. When it comes to a trading system associated with the automated trading refers to the gill of trading that studies and implements the algorithms, which may lead to the market trading operations in automatic mode without needing human intervention. You have real robots that have been programmed by the trader to do the job instead.

So, these robots, as such, should completely eliminate the emotional part of the financial markets?

Not at all, in fact, I believe that the emotional aspect is also valid in the era of algo-trading, as the trading system (automated trading systems, programs/robot that can trade in place of man after they have been programmed with precise setup) they are still designed and calibrated by humans. Ergo emotions may persist even in systems.

The fact remains that today we live in the digital age and the age of the algorithm, this is also valid in the field of trading and investments. So, the knowledge of these new tools turns out to be indispensable. Be aware of the factors, such as tools, psychology and behavior is always useful in each investment area. Both in the case of private traders in the case of institutional investors, behind every trading operation, there is always the reasoning of one or more people, but above all, their emotions.

In this regard, it is useful to remember that emotions are obviously irrational. Often it is emotions that are the cause of actions, in our case, the reason for a buy or sell operation on the financial markets. So, the fundamental analysis of the markets becomes very useful for long-term operations (temporal order of months or years), while short-term operations, which are at the mercy of the operator's emotions, could escape this kind of control. Having said that, one of the key tools that should be studied and known is:

Calendar of Economic Events and Basic Data

The calendar is always available online every day of the week and regularly publishes important data, this tool can be displayed and used on different channels of dissemination of economic news, and usually, it's a tool that can be enjoyed for free. An example of an economic calendar is shown below:

Time	Cur.	Imp.	Event	Actual	Forecast	Previous
05:00	EUR	▼	Core CPI (MoM) (Dec)	0.4%	0.4%	0.4%
05:00	EUR	▼ ▼	CPI (MoM) (Dec)	0.3%	0.3%	-0.3%
05:00	EUR	▼ ▼ ▼	CPI (YoY) (Dec)	1.3%	1.3%	1.3%
05:00	EUR	▼	CPI ex Tobacco (MoM) (Dec)	0.3%		-0.4%
05:00	EUR	▼	CPI ex Tobacco (YoY) (Dec)	1.2%		0.9%
05:00	EUR	▼	HICP ex Energy & Food (YoY) (Dec)	1.4%	1.4%	1.4%
05:00	EUR	▼	HICP ex Energy and Food (MoM) (Dec)	0.3%	0.3%	-0.4%
2 min	INR	▼	Bank Loan Growth			7.1%
2 min	INR	▼	Deposit Growth			10.1%
2 min	INR	▼	FX Reserves, USD			461.16B
08:00	RUB	▼	Trade Balance (Nov)			12.42B
08:30	USD	▼ ▼ ▼	Building Permits (Dec)		1.468M	1.474M
08:30	USD	▼ ▼	Building Permits (MoM) (Dec)			0.9%
08:30	USD	▼ ▼	Housing Starts (Dec)		1.375M	1.365M
08:30	USD	▼ ▼	Housing Starts (MoM) (Dec)			3.2%
08:30	CAD	▼ ▼	Foreign Securities Purchases (Nov)			11.32B
08:30	CAD	▼	Foreign Securities Purchases by Canadians (Nov)			2.03B
09:00	USD	▼ ▼	FOMC Member Harker Speaks			
09:15	USD	▼	Capacity Utilization Rate (Dec)		77.1%	77.3%
09:15	USD	▼ ▼	Industrial Production (MoM) (Dec)		-0.2%	1.1%

Image 13: In the image, an example of an economic calendar. The table shows the columns for the time of publication of the news (or data), the currency, then the country concerned for the news published, the impact that the news may have differentiated in the image table with the number of heads of bull. The columns of the table proceed with the type and name of the event, the data of the past publication for the same event, the value expected by the analysts, and finally, the current published value. The image was created using the economic information website courtesy on Investing.

As I mentioned in the lines prior to the image, the economic calendar can be found on different distribution channels, including online. This is the first concrete tool that allows you to follow the economic news of the financial markets.

I invite the reader to look now at the keyword "economic calendar," enter the various sites that offer free of this type of service and to become familiar with this tool, recalling the fact that the calendar of economic and fundamental data news accompany the activity of the trader for life. The investing site is not the only supplier of real-time data; in fact, using a search engine like Google, you can quickly get other free providers about the news. The reader's attention should be focused on the possibility of using the instrument of the information for their own personal trading; following each operator will use the news site they prefer to use the economic calendar.

- The publication date and time of the data
- The place or nation interested in that news
- The more or less significant impact that the news has on the markets
- The type of event affected by the data
- The past value for that particular data, which can be a number or a percentage
- The expected value, therefore the expectation of analysts and operators

When important economic news is published that has a great emotional and functional impact on the market, this usually generates an increase in volatility or a large "swing" in prices. This can lead to quick and sudden gains, and in the same way, to impetuous and painful losses.

Reading the fundamental data, it is necessary to take into consideration the anticipatory characteristics of the market; that is, the price may increase pending data that is presumed to be positive. Subsequently, the price may drop approaching the old levels. This depends a lot on the expectations that are had for that type of news, therefore also on the value foreseen by the economic calendar. This is obviously not a fixed rule. The prior sentence could be simplified with the following:

"Buy when the trading community expects a positive result and sell when the news becomes public."

But as always in the trading and investment, this is not a fixed rule that can always work, otherwise, it would be far too easy to become rich by trading on the stock exchange. The Online Trading on financial markets is one of the methods used to achieve Financial Freedom; in fact, once you learn the mechanisms that are behind this business system, it is also possible to use operability that requires little time. This turns out to be valid in relation to the structuring operations that build private trader for his business. In addition, today, it is possible to entrust the operation of your trading account to automatic algorithms, robots that can be produced by the trader or that can be purchased by professional experts in the sector.

It is not easy to make money with trading given that this is an activity that requires constant updating and deepening, this type of activity may not be suitable for all, but the fact remains that with trading, you can really make a lot of money! The aspect that makes the difference is that the information, I am not referring to the information on which tool to buy or sell (the so-called "inside information"), but to training and personal knowledge. In the era of the information revolution, therefore, the digital revolution, the time and resources spent on training are the ones that get the best performance. In fact, courses and books offer a competitive advantage made the difference between those who can and those who cannot do a certain thing.

CHAPTER 7:

Technical Analysis

Technical analysis can be defined simply as a method, process, or tool that is used by investors to predict and foretell a stock's price movement based on data from the markets.

We can also define technical analysis of trends and stocks as the analysis of past market data that includes volume and price. The main purpose of the analysis is to obtain information that helps in predicting expected market behavior. Traders and investors believe strongly that precious stock price is a reliable indicator of future performance.

There is a notion that supports technical analysis. Apparently, the sale and purchase of stocks at the markets collectively by traders, investors, and other players is accurately manifested in the security. This holds then that technical analysis provides a fair and relatively accurate market price to a stock or any other security.

Purpose of technical analysis

The main purpose of technical analysis is to foretell the expected price movements of stocks and trends and to provide relevant information to investors, traders, and other market players to enable them to trade profitably.

As a swing trader, you will apply technical analysis to the various charts that you will be using. You will use different tools on the charts so as to determine what the potential entry and exit points for a particular trade are.

Factors Affecting Technical Analysis

Technical analysis can be applied to numerous securities, including Forex, stocks, futures, commodities, indices, and many more. The price of a security depends on a collection of metrics. These are volume, low, open, high, close, open interest, and so on. These are also known as market action or price data.

There are a couple of assumptions that we make as traders when performing the technical analysis. However, remember that it is applicable only in situations where the price is only a factor of demand and supply. Should there be other factors that can influence prices significantly, then the technical analysis will not work. The following assumptions are often made about securities that are being analyzed.

There are no artificial price movements: Artificial price movements are usually as a result of distributions, dividends, and splits. Such changes in stock price can greatly alter the price chart, and this tends to cause technical analysis to be very difficult to implement. Fortunately, it is possible to remedy this.

All that you need to do as an analyst is to make adjustments to historical data before the price changes.

The stock is highly liquid: Another major assumption that the technical analysis makes is that the stock is highly liquid. Liquidity is absolutely crucial for volumes. When stocks are heavily traded as a result of liquidity and volume, then traders are able to easily enter and exit trades. Stocks that are not highly traded tend to be rather difficult to trade because there are very few sellers and buyers at any point in time. Also, stocks with low liquidity are usually poorly priced, sometimes at less than a penny for each share. This is risky as they can be manipulated by investors.

Trend: If you are interested in trading based on trend, then what you are looking to do is follow the crowd when it comes to trading and make a profit on volume along with everyone else. Trend can either move up or down, with indicators of an upward trend include above-average lows with a downward trend, including lower than average highs. Regardless of the trend that is occurring, the earlier that you can determine what it is, the more you can profit from its overall.

At that point, you should find holding onto your chosen position is a relatively simple matter up until the point where the trend heads back in the opposite direction. Due to the fact that a trend trader is never going to really know when it is going to reverse on them, it is important to ensure that you always use stops that are extremely controlled in order to ensure your profits don't vanish at the first signs of a reversing trend.

This type of trading is often going to generate a far greater number of losing trades than other strategies, though the individual gains are likely going to be larger in nature as well. This, in turn, means that if you do not feel as though you want to deal with a lot of risk management issues, then you will likely feel more comfortable trading based on range instead. A trade that is made based on following the trend should never be more than two percent of the total amount of capital you plan on trading with. Furthermore, it is important to keep your liquidity in mind to make sure you don't end up in over your head unexpectedly. Keep in mind that it will almost always be a better choice to take a smaller profit in the moment rather than risking it all on something that could knock you out of the game completely.

Understand core assumptions: The technical analysis is all about measuring the relative value of a particular trade or underlying asset by using available tools to find otherwise invisible patterns that, ideally, few other people have currently noticed. When it comes to using the technical analysis properly, you are going to always need to assume three things are true. First and foremost, the market ultimately discounts everything; second, trends will always be an adequate predictor of price, and third, history is bound to repeat itself when given enough time to do so.

Technical analysis believes that the current price of a specific underlying asset is the only true metric that matters when it comes to considering the current state of tings both in the market and outside it. This is due to the fact that everything else about the market has already been factored through the price to get it to where it is now, which means that analyzing it, when compared to the overall state of the market, should provide you all of the information you need.

Additionally, the technical analysis holds to be true the fact that the current value of an underlying asset moves based on the trend that has been established, which means it can be tracked as long as you know what to look for. What this means is that once a trend has been identified, then it is really just a matter of waiting for it to come around again before you can take advantage of it. Statistically speaking, it is always more likely that a trend is going to repeat than a new trend is going to form out of nowhere or a trend is going to reverse dramatically instead.

CHAPTER 8:

Technical Indicators

Indicators of Trade

This is a measure or gauge of trade that allows analyzing prices and provides trade signals. Indicators provide trade signals that alert a trader when it is time to trade. Day trading indicators are not to be used as the only plan. They should be used along with a well laid out though, to make it a useful trading tool. No matter the kind of trade one is involved in, having many trading indicators may bring inconsistency with trading decisions due to the complexities involved. Keeping it simple could simply be the trick to making clear and less stressful trading decisions.

Trading indicators should not, therefore, be taken as the only method relied on trading. However, using indicators alongside other trading variables may come in handy. Getting rid of the many indicators helps traders have a simplistic approach to the market.

Role of Technical Indicators

- Get the direction trend
- Determine the momentum or lack of momentum in the market
- Determine if and if not, the market is growing

- Get the volume to determine how popular a market is with traders

Getting the same type of indicators that on the chart that give the same information is where the issue is. This is because you may give conflicting information or get more information than you may be stressful. The main shortcoming of most indicators is that since they are gotten from price, they delay the price. There are rules that one can use to determine useful indicators for day trading, swing trading, and position trading. This include, among others:

- Choosing one trend indicator such as moving average and one momentum trading indicator is the simplest rule.

- Knowing well the perimeters you want to investigate before you decide on the trading indicators which you will use on your charts. Then know well the indicator you chose in terms of how it works, calculations it does and the effects it will bring for your trading decisions.

- Indicators work only depending on how they are incorporated into the trading plan. Some indicators like MACD and CCI are best at calculating information. Others like alligator indicator are fast at showing a market that is trending and ranging. Other indicators will show directions and act as entry and exit signals of trade. The usage of a basic indicator along with a well laid out trading plan by back, forward and demo can you put you ahead of trade with many complicated indicators. Netpicks offers systems that test trade plans, prove trading systems and trading indicators.

Threat of Optimization

There is a hindrance or barriers for when one is searching for trading indicators that work for one's style and trading plan. Most systems sell standard indicators that are fine-tuned to show successful results from the past. This is a disadvantage since it does not take into account the market changes. Using the standard settings for all indicators help avoid over-optimization trap which helps a trader not to focus on today's market progress and miss on the future.

Best Technical Trading Indicators

For day trading, a trader should test several indicators individually then later as a combination. One may end up with say 3-5 good ones that are evergreen and decide to switch off depending on the market at that particular day or the asset trading.

Regardless of the type of trade, day, Forex or futures the idea is to keep it simple with the indicators. Use one indicator per category to avoid repeating the same thing and distraction.

Combining Indicators

Combining pairs of indicators on the price chart helps to identify points to initiate trade. A good example is a combination of RSI and moving average convergence which combined suggest and reinforce a trading signal. When choosing sets it's important to find one indicator considered a leading indicator and another that is a lagging indicator. Leading indicators show signals before the forms for entering trade has been made. Lagging indicators on the other hand show signals after the formation have happened. Therefore, lagging indicators can confirm leading indicators and help a trader from trading on wrong signals. Choosing a combination of pairs that include indicators of different types instead of the same type is highly advisable. It does not make sense to observe a combination of the same type of indicators because they will still give the same information.

Multiple Indicators

Using multiple indicators boosts trading signals and may increase chances of telling out false signals.

Refining Indicators

Knowing the weaknesses of an indicator to determine if it gives a lot of false signals, if sometimes it fails to signal or if it signals too late or too early is essential. Knowing these things about the indicator will help determine what the indicator is best suited for. You may find that the indicator is suited for Forex instead of stocks while you thought it was just ineffective. This might help you decide if you want to trade the indicator for another or to just simply change how it's calculated. Doing this refining, will help an indicator work best for you, and also for you to find the best indicator for different types of trading.

CHAPTER 9:

Finding Undervalued Stocks

You need to perform three fundamental steps in order to find undervalued stocks:

• Perform a preliminary evaluation of several stocks to see if they meet your investment criteria;

• Based on your preliminary evaluation, develop a shortlist of stocks that you want to further examine and evaluate; and

• Perform a more detailed investigation of your shortlisted stocks by closely inspecting the companies' financial information.

The internet has actually made it a lot easier for investors to acquire the free financial information of companies they are interested in investing. There are many websites now, such as Edgars and Sedar that offer extensive databases of financial data, including audited financial statements, press releases, corporate reports, stock prices, and earnings per share.

However, given the barrage of information, how will you know if a particular stock is currently being sold below its inherent worth? Here are just two of the financial ratios that you should look at to assess a particular stock's inherent worth:

- **Price/Earnings (P/E) Ratio**

You will soon hear financial analysts say that a particular stock is currently selling for "x-times earnings"–20-times earnings or 10.5-times earnings. This means that the stock's current market price is currently selling at 20 times higher than the earnings per share of the company. The goal is to find stocks with very low P/E ratios because that means that those companies are selling their stocks at lower prices.

- **Earnings Yield**

Earnings yield is basically the opposite of P/E ratio. Therefore, a company with a 20-times earnings (P/E ratio) has a 1/20 or 5% earnings yield. If value investors are looking for low P/E ratios, the opposite applies with earnings yield (i.e., Value investors are looking for stocks with higher earnings yield compared to other companies within the same industry).

In addition to the quantitative assessments mentioned above, you must also perform qualitative assessments that allow you to better understand the intrinsic value of a particular company.

One of these qualitative assessments is the evaluation of the company's "insider purchasing activity?" You want to know what the company's executives (senior managers, officers, directors and other major stockholders) are doing with their stock ownerships.

These insiders, especially the senior managers and the board of directors, have "inside" information about the operations of their own company. Therefore, if you see them aggressively buying their company's stock, you can reasonably presume that the company's operations are moving towards a favorable future.

However, don't jump to quick conclusions when you see an insider selling his or her stock ownership. It does not always mean that the company is heading towards bankruptcy or harder times. For all you know, that particular director or senior manager is in dire need of extra cash to fund his or her personal expenditures. You can, however, begin to doubt the company's future prospects if many of the insiders begin to sell most of their stock ownerships. When you observe that scenario, you need to perform further investigations to see if the company is heading towards difficult times.

Now, you may ask, "How will I know when a company's board of directors or senior management is buying or selling their stocks?" Don't worry because the Securities and Exchange Commission (SEC) has made it easier for investors to know about this information. Insiders are obligated to report their purchasing activities to the SEC within 2 business days after the transaction. You can then freely access this information through the official SEC website.

The Essence of Value Investing

As we mentioned earlier, you need to have the eagerness to do some serious reading and investigations if you want to be successful in value investing.

You do not really need to have a degree in finance and accounting, but it will greatly help if you make the effort to learn about basic accounting so that you can more properly analyze and interpret financial statements. Remember that you do not make a decision to buy a particular stock because its financial ratios look promising or because you recently learned that its current market price has considerably dropped. In order to determine whether a particular stock is a good buy or not, you have to rely on more than simply taking in everything you see at face value. You will need to use your common sense and your critical thinking skills in order to be successful.

Beyond the financial ratios and the insider purchasing activity, you need to spend some time to ask the following questions and to find the answers:

- How do you think the company's operations will look like five years, ten years, or even twenty years from now?
- Will the company be able to continuously increase its revenues either by selling more or by increasing their prices?
- Will the company be able to sustain an efficient operation by making sure that costs of goods sold and operating expenses are strictly controlled?
- How often do they sell or close down divisions or subsidiaries that do not make any profit?

- How strong is the company within their industry? Are they one of the market leaders? Do they have stronger competitors?

As you become more experienced, you will know what other questions you need to ask. Once you have the answers, you use these together with the financial ratios and insider purchasing activities to determine whether a particular stock is a good buy or not.

To improve your chances to succeed in value investing, it is advisable to purchase stocks from companies that you understand. This is the strategy that helped Warren Buffett earn millions from his stock investments. If you have always worked in the airline industry, you can say that you have a good working knowledge of that industry and the companies within it. Because you normally buy clothes, grocery items, and household appliances, you most probably have basic knowledge about the retail industry.

Another technique that successful value investors utilize is to purchase stocks of companies that have been producing products or rendering services for a long time and there is a very high probability that their products or services will continue to be in demand. You cannot identify these companies simply by analyzing their financial information. You will have to perform some critical thinking to determine which companies fall under this category. Let's take the Coca-Cola Company as an example. Coke products have been widely accepted worldwide for several decades now and many people believe that these products will continue to be in demand for a very long time. You can look at other companies you are familiar with and see how they have adapted over time. It is also ideal if you can perform an analysis of the management style of the companies to see how effective their corporate governance is in ensuring that the companies can thrive during both good times and bad times.

Remember, value investors invest for the long-term; they do not make haphazard and random investment decisions. They take their time in studying and investigating a particular company before they use their capital to purchase stocks. It is never enough to just browse through the stock market prices and read quick commentaries from financial analysts.

CHAPTER 10:

Who are Your Partners?

You need to open an account with the broker before you can invest in the stock market. The issue is that with all the brokers out there encouraging you to sign up and make an investment, how do you determine the broker that can best match your needs? Make sure that your broker passes this basic so that you will have the finest investing or stock trading experience.

Banking

Make sure you check the methods of depositing, as well as the methods of withdrawal. It is not unusual to find brokers who use more options when making a deposit but only have limited choices when making a withdrawal.

A broker would typically require you to send a copy of your identity files before you even begin your withdrawal. Take note of how many days it will take for your broker to process your payment in full from the time you make a withdrawal request.

Minimum Deposit and Withdrawal Limit Please notice that a minimum deposit is required. Some brokers require a minimum deposit of $250, while others may find a minimal deposit of only $25. You will also need to learn the minimum and maximum withdrawal limits. A broker may charge a small fee as well as a withdrawal charge, which is normal. If you plan to make numerous withdrawals in a week, then the withdrawal charge is something that you ought to pay attention to.

Demo Account

Your broker must provide you with a complimentary demo account. This is an excellent method to get a feel of actual trading in a real-time stock market environment without risking any money.

Charges

These fees are usually a small amount; they can pile up rapidly, particularly if you make plenty of trades in a short time. Be sure to compare the different brokers that you find online and look for the one that offers the lowest fees.

Trading Platform

Every online broker will offer you with a trading platform where you can buy and offer stocks with just a couple of clicks of a mouse. Your broker ought to provide you with a professionally created platform with useful features. The finest brokers will provide you with a complimentary data or details about the stock market to assist you in making the most excellent financial investment decision. Your broker must likewise provide you with graphs and charts in case you wish to use the technical analysis.

Trading Restrictions

Your broker must not limit how you trade, in addition to just how much you can trade. Some brokers will require you first to contact them before you purchase stocks using the site as if you need approval from them for any investment that you make. Some brokers will even place restrictions on the number of stocks that you can sell or buy. You must keep away from these brokers. You ought to only work with a broker that will permit you to make a financial investment on your own. It must likewise allow you to trade lots of stocks as you desire.

Trust Rating, of course, you require to work only with a broker that is trusted and reputable. Once you sign up for an account with any broker, make sure to check the feedback made by other investors. A simple way to do this easily is to use your favorite internet browser, key the name of the broker in the search bar, and just include the word ratings. Hit the Enter key, and you will discover a list of pages that will most likely have the evaluations on your selected broker.

Likewise, focus on the dates when the current comments were done. If the most recent favorable evaluations were made about a year earlier, then be careful. The management team and even the strategy of the broker will vary from time to time.

Mobile Feature

The broker will also provide you with a mobile platform. This ensures that you should be able to manage the portfolio and save by just using your mobile phone.

When you use a desktop computer,—and the process should be as convenient as you are. Do not fret; brokers with a high score always have a mobile function. Having a mobile option is one of the reasons that people like individual brokers.

Consumer Support

Test if the broker has a live chat option on the web. If the broker can only be reached by e-mail, then check how easily the broker can respond and pay attention to how efficient the broker can treat the order. Preferably, the consumer assistance ought to be able to meet with a response to your questions within 24 hours!

CHAPTER 11:

Buying Your First Stock

I n spite of the higher-than-normal instability, when you buy stock and gain the legitimate option to take an interest in the profits and losses of the undertaking, your money can develop such that just is preposterous with securities, authentications of the store, or at times, even land. For the beginners, one of the more typical inquiries posed includes how to buy stock; the mechanics of really getting your hands on that bit of proprietorship qualifying you for dividends that are immediately stored or sent to your family so you can appreciate the surge of passive income.

There are a few distinct approaches to buy stock, each with its own focal points and hindrances, including assessment and liquidity contemplations. Some well-known options can assist you with increasing the general format of the land and be better educated to settle on choices of value securing.

The most effective method to Buy Stock in a Regular, Taxable Brokerage Account

In the event that you need to buy stock without any limitations, no favorable duty circumstances, and no commitment restrains, the most effortless route is to open a brokerage account. Picking a particular brokerage house includes a few contemplations, for example, regardless of whether you need a full-administration broker or a rebate broker that does simply executing your stock exchanges at absolute bottom costs, however nowadays it is as simple as taking five minutes to round out a progression of inquiries on the web.

Envision you needed to open a record at Charles Schwab and Company, probably the greatest broker in the United States. You would round out the online application, giving your name, address, government disability number, work data, and all the more relying on whether you needed to include edge obligation capacity or stock option trading benefits. You would then send in the base record equalization of $1,000 or, on the other hand, pursue $100 every month direct stores or electronic scopes from a Schwab financial records.

When your brokerage account had been opened, you would see the money stored and stopped, hanging tight for you to accomplish something with it. You would sign on to the site, enter the ticker image of the organization you needed to buy, enter the quantity of shares you expected to purchase, and present the exchange a couple of snaps once you had checked the subtleties. By and large, inside a second or two, you'd see the stock saved into your record and the money pulled back. A couple of days after the fact, you'd get an exchange affirmation archive.

At whatever point the organization delivered a profit, you'd see it direct stored into your brokerage account. On the off chance that the organization at any point had a tax-exempt side project or split-off, you'd see those shares saved into your brokerage account, also (e.g., Chipotle Mexican Grill was separated from McDonald's while Allstate Insurance was spun-off from Sears).

The most effective method to Buy Stock in a Roth IRA, Traditional IRA, SIMPLE IRA, SEP-IRA or Other Similar Retirement Account.

From the point of a stray piece of view, the way toward buying stock in a Roth IRA, for all intents and purposes indistinguishable from buying stock in a standard, assessable brokerage account. In the event that your IRA is held at a brokerage firm, you follow precisely the same methodology. The distinction has to do with how the charges are dealt with and the measure of new money you can contribute every year.

For instance, you can possibly contribute $5,500 to a Traditional IRA in the event that you are 49 years of age or more youthful, and $6,500 on the off chance that you are 50 years old or more established. For whatever length of time that you fall beneath as far as possible as a result for the year dependent on your conjugal status, you can discount these commitments as though you never brought in the money. In the interim, the dividends and capital pick up your money gains while investing in stock inside the Traditional IRA are totally tax-exempt with just a bunch of special cases. At the point when you go to haul the money out of the record, you pay a customary income charge on the sum pulled back.

In the event that you attempt to pull back the money too soon, you'll be dependent upon a 10% punishment charge except if you meet one of the eight exclusion.

The most effective method to Buy Stock through a Direct Stock Purchase Plan or Dividend Reinvestment Plan (otherwise known as DRIP).

Imagine where you would prefer not to open a brokerage account. You're in karma. Numerous companies, particularly enormous blue-chip shares, support programs that permit you to buy stock straightforwardly from the company's exchange specialist for nothing, or at an intensely financed cost. Consider the advanced relative of John D. Rockefeller's oil realm, Exxon Mobil. It supports an immediate stock buy plan through a business called Computershare. Would-be proprietors who open a record with either $250 or consent to having $50 every month pulled back from a checking or bank account can buy the stock at no commission. Surprisingly better, the arrangement permits partial stock buys so each and every penny gets set to work for you, the investor, regardless of whether you don't have precisely the perfect add up to obtain a full offer at some random time.

At the point when you apply on the web, you can tell the exchange specialist whether you need your dividends direct saved into your checking or bank account or reinvested in extra shares of stock. Choose cautiously. While there is no set-in-stone answer—everything relies upon your own budgetary circumstance and the resulting execution of the stock itself—there is a major contrast among reinvesting and not reinvesting your dividends over extensive stretches of time in case you're lucky enough to wind up possessing a really extraordinary endeavor.

CHAPTER 12:

Selling Time

Selling a stock at the correct time is also equally important. The whole point of keeping a close watch of your selected stocks is to remain fully aware of their performance in the market. It is a fact that in the long-term, the companies with strong fundamentals usually perform well. The reason is very simple; the companies are inclined to grow. There is a complete system that is trying to make a profit and, as a result, even your money invested in that stock makes a profit.

However, this may not be the case for every business venture. There can be times when a company that has been doing everything right starts to move on a downward curve. There can be many reasons for the downfall of the company.

The descent on the path of self-destruction can be caused by management issues. Various government regulations and restrictions can also make the functioning of that company difficult. From long and slanderous litigations to better products in the market, the reasons for the downfall of a company can be many.

As an investor, it is your responsibility to keep a close watch on your investment. You will have to remain in the loop of the news relating to that segment and that company in particular.

First – The Value Judgment

Once you realize that the value of the stock might go down or has already started to go down, it is important that you make the decision of exiting the stock and squaring off your position at the earliest possible.

Here, it is very important that your decision to exit a stock must not be a knee-jerk reaction. You must understand that many people try to square off their positions in a fundamentally sound company at the first news of anything bad about the company. Many a time there is nothing substantial about such gossip and the companies come out of the initial shock reaction very fast. But, if you try to exit a stock when many other investors are also trying to do the same, you will be looking at a major loss. Remember, the market works on a demand and supply rule.

If the fundamentals of the company are strong and still the prices of a stock are coming down due to some random news or market manipulation, such times are good for buying and not for selling.

But, in the case, you have a strong reason to believe that there is something wrong with the fundamentals of the company or something is happening which might damage the prospects of the company in the long-run, it would be wise to make an early exit before the market gets panic-stricken. Your decision should not be emotional but financial in nature.

Second – The Order Judgement

The next thing to do is to judge the type of order you want to place. Like buying, you can place the orders too as a market order and limit order.

Market Order: In case you suspect there is something very wrong with the company, and there is a chance that panic like situation may arise, it is good to make an early exit. Through market order, you will be able to square off all your positions in that stock at the market rate and wouldn't have to wait for long.

If you have placed your order in the 'after hours,' the order will get executed at the start of the next business day at the prevailing rates.

You will have no control over the rates in such a situation, and whatever the rate at the time of opening will be, your orders will get executed at that price.

Limit Order: You can place this type of order if you don't feel that there is anything wrong with the company but want to book your profits for some other reason. The limit order option gives you better control over the price you'll get.

When you place your sell order, you may also have to fill other details in the trade portal as well.

The required details would be:

Quantity: The number of shares you want to sell. Here, you can choose to square off your complete position or rebalance your stock position a little by selling off a few stocks in this firm. Fill in the exact number of shares you want to sell.

Order Type: In this part, you will have to fill the kind of order you would like this to be. This means you want to place a market order or a limit order.

Time in Force or Order Expiration: The next thing that you would have to put will be the 'time in force' or order expiration. This clearly states the period of time for which your order would be valid.

This is a feature put in place to give you better control.

The various terms you may come across in it are:

Day: This means your specific order can be good for the day, and you might want to have a different price or strategy for the next day. If you place this order and the trade doesn't get executed the same day, you will have to place a big again on the next market opening.

Good till Cancelled: You can also place an order that's good for as long as it takes to execute that order or before you cancel it. This gives you freedom from placing the bid again and again for that stock.

Immediate or Cancel: You can also place an order under this category to dump your holdings in that stock immediately. However, any part of the order that remains unfulfilled will automatically stand canceled, and you will have to place a bid on it again and if you want to square it off.

Fill or Kill: This type of order is placed if you want to square off a large position all at once. You can place an order, and this will only get executed if your complete position in that stock is getting squared off.

On the Open: This type of order will get executed at the opening of the market. You will not have any specific control over the price on which it gets filled. It will be highly dependent on the sentiment about that stock price at the market opening.

On the Close: This type of order will get settled at the price prevailing at the time of the market close.

CHAPTER 13:

Stock Scanning and Creating a Watch List

You can only scan through stocks as fast as you can type them into your terminal. This delay in receiving information will often lead to missed opportunities, which could have provided great profits had you only seen the setup unfolding early enough.

You are highly encouraged to use this functionality as it can identify profitable trade opportunities early enough for you to take advantage of them. The code I will provide is central to the ThinkOrSwim platform, however, the concepts will remain the same regardless of what analysis software you are using. I encourage you to read the content, understand why I am setting up my filters the way I am, and apply the principles it to your own trading style.

The first step in developing any sort of scanning functionality is first to create a well-built watch list of stocks that you may be interested in trading.

As of writing this, there are currently 230 stocks on my watch list. Each of these stocks has been hand-selected to have the appropriate factors in place, which make them easy to trade. I look for things such as volume, volatility, and stability when it comes to trading a stock. If the volume is low, it will be difficult for you to get in and out of positions; the higher the volume of the stock, the easier it is to open a new position or hand off existing shares to someone else. I will typically only trade stocks whose average volume over a 14-period range is 800k shares traded or greater.

The next thing I look for is volatility. The definition of volatility in terms of financial securities is their liability to change. Volatile stocks will have wide price swings allowing for greater profit potential, while non-volatile stocks will trade in a very tight price range, making it difficult to extract large profits. To measure volatility, I use the Average True Range (ATR) of a stock. ATR is simply the average difference between a stock's low and high of the day over a given period (I use 14 trading periods to measure ATR). It is important to remember that ATR is not a static variable and changes every day, stocks move in cycles where their ATR goes from low values to higher values back to low values—usually corresponding with volume. As a rule of thumb, I will only trade stocks where the ATR is 2% or greater. Which means, in any time, the difference between the low price and high price of the trading day will be 2% or more.

The final thing I look for is stability. I define stability much differently than most people do. When I look for stability, I am really talking about the Bid-Ask spread. A stable stock will have a reasonable Bid-Ask spread, meanwhile an un-stable stock will be more susceptible to manipulation and will have a very large bid-ask spread. Stocks such as AAPL, which are trading in the

$120 price range have a relatively small bid-ask spread–typically $0.10 difference between the Bid price and the Ask price. I call this stable. There are other stocks out there that are trading at $8 and have spreads where the Bid is $7.10 and the Ask is $9.15. This is not a stable stock as it has a very wide Bid-Ask spread. It ultimately falls on you to decide what you constitute as a "stable" stock.

Now that our watch list is created, we want to set up our scan filters. Use the following code in ThinkOrSwim to scan for stocks where a squeeze has fired off (this is done in the Scan tab):

```
BollingerBandsSMA()."lowerband"          >
KeltnerChannels()."lower_band"           and
BollingerBandsSMA()."lowerband"          <
KeltnerChannels()."lower_band"
```

Running a scan with these parameters will return stocks that have just fired off a squeeze. I run this scan on a Daily chart as I typically swing trade, however, the same code can be applied on a 1 minute or 5-minute aggregation period for people who day trade.

By running this code via the Scan tab, you are able to automatically scan the markets for squeezes and find profitable trading opportunities. It negates the need to be constantly looking at charts searching for an entry. For those who want to scan for stocks that are currently in a squeeze (red dots on the TTM Squeeze histogram) you can use the following lines of code instead:

BollingerBandsSMA()."Upperband"   <
KeltnerChannels()."Upper_band"   or
BollingerBandsSMA()."lowerband"   >
KeltnerChannels()."lower_band"

This scan query will result in ThinkOrSwim returning a list of stocks that are still in a squeeze that hasn't fired off yet. It is an excellent way to find stocks where you can get into a squeeze trade early before it has actually fired off.

The next filter I add to my scan query will look for a positive TTM Wave value. I do this because with current market conditions I am primarily focused on looking for bullish squeeze trade setups. In order to scan for a positive TTM Wave, I use the following code:

def hist = reference TTM_Squeeze.Histogram;

def w1 = reference TTM_Wave.Wave1;

def w2h = reference TTM_Wave.Wave2High;

def w2l = reference TTM_Wave.Wave2Low;

plot scan = w1 < 0 and w2h < 0 and w2l < 0;

This code is running twice, on both a weekly and a daily timeframe in order to automatically find stocks which are in a squeeze, have a positive wave on the daily chart, and have a positive wave on the weekly chart (our anchor chart). When all done, this is what my filters look like in Thinkorswim:

At this point, trading is a matter of running your scan to automatically find trade setups for you to take, setting effective price targets using Elliott Lines, and then taking the trade.

There is one additional rule that I will follow when trading stocks: I will never trade a stock either 2 weeks before or 2 weeks after it has announced earnings or dividends. While this may seem overly-cautious to some, I follow this rule in an effort to reduce risk. During earnings season, stocks can become extremely volatile to the point where even the best technical indicators fail.

CHAPTER 14:

Day and Swing Trading

Now we are going to look at a short-term strategy used to earn cash in the here and now, rather than investing in companies for long term growth. These strategies take advantage of the short-term changes in the stock price in order to realize profits.

The two methods:

Day Trading: When you day trade, you buy and sell the same security on the same trading day. This is a highly regulated activity. A brokerage will determine that you are a day trader if you execute 4-day trades within any 5-business day period (that makes you a "Pattern Day Trader"). To be a day trader, most brokerages require you to have $25,000 in your account. There are a few firms that will let you day trade with small accounts, but they charge large commissions. As a result, those companies are used by new day traders without much capital to learn, but experienced traders use regular brokerages so that they can avoid the high fees.

Swing Trading: this is a lower risk strategy. This is simply a buy-low and sell-high strategy that can last any time length you want but up to a maximum of a few months. A swing trader doesn't day trade, so at a minimum, a swing trader will hold an investment overnight. Swing trading is a much lower risk unless the company goes bankrupt or there is a huge recession (and hopefully you are doing your research so that you know what is possible) the stock is probably going to go higher than what you paid for it at some point in the near future. Since its lower risk, swing trading has no capital requirements.

Despite the differences, the techniques used are the same. Day trading is considered a high-risk activity, higher risk than swing trading, and much higher risk than normal stock investing. It's hard to say that swing trading is really that high risk as compared to buying shares of an individual stock for any purpose. If it's not profitable to sell, the swing trader can just hang on to the stock.

Goals and Risks

The goal of day traders and swing traders is to make cash profits. So, you can think of it as a trading business rather than acting as an investor. You are more concerned with the short-term fluctuations in stock price than you are with the long-term prospects of the company. For the day trader, they are looking at profiting off of price fluctuations that happen over the course of hours, minutes, and even seconds. A swing trader is looking to take advantage of price swings in the share price that occur over periods of days, weeks, or even several months.

One risk, especially with day trading, is that emotion will take hold. This can happen with positive and negative emotions. So, you might have too much fear of loss and get out too early, or you might get greedy and not sell when you should because you have dreams of the share price skyrocketing.

Another risk is new traders don't use standard methods of mitigating risk that can minimize loss of capital when your speculations go wrong. One problem is many people simply jump on and start trading without really knowing what is going on. Instead, you should take the time to invest in yourself and take some courses on day trading from professionals.

Potential gains

Most new day traders will probably lose money, at least at first. However, if you've put the time in to study and done some practice, including taking a course, you might be on the way to becoming a successful day trader. Those that are successful can make high annual incomes.

Risk Mitigating Steps

Let's look at some important risk-mitigating steps you must take in order to successfully day trade without losing all your capital.

Clear Sell Criteria

If you are looking to profit off the rise in a stock price, then have a specific target in mind and sell when it reaches the target. Let's say you buy shares of a given stock at $10 a share, and it starts rising. You set a profit target at $15 a share. When it hits that, you sell it and book your profits, and you don't let emotion get the best of you and fret if it does up to $20 a share. A greedy trader or one who gets overly excited might hold the stock too long, hoping it will just keep rising. But then suddenly it might drop back down to even a lower level than what they paid for it. You should have a profit target in mind when you buy your shares and stick to it no matter what happens.

Putting a daily limit

You can also help protect yourself by putting a daily limit on the amount of capital you're willing to risk each day. So maybe you only allow yourself to buy $3,000 worth of shares (or whatever) so that you're not betting the farm.

Avoid trading on the margin

Using margin trading (borrowing money from the broker) is where a lot of people get themselves into financial trouble. If you don't spend what you don't have, then you can avoid getting in trouble in the first place. Instead of letting yourself get emotional about some supposedly "sure thing," have a steady plan for profits that you earn over the course of time, rather than hoping that you've "found the big thing" and you're going to possibly get yourself in huge trouble by borrowing a lot of money to realize your dreams, when the odds are solid your predictions will be wrong.

Calculating risk

Let's look at how advisors recommend you calculate your risk. The risk on a single trade should be 1% of the capital in your account. Let's say that shares of a given stock are trading at $100 and you have an account with $50,000. So, 1% of $50,000 is $500. That means the most you can risk is $500, but that doesn't apply to the total amount spent on buying the shares, so you don't buy $500 worth of shares. What it means is that you put a stop-loss order to limit your total loss to $500. So, if you put a stop-loss order at $99, that is a $1 loss per share, so you could buy 500 shares. So, you could risk your entire $50,000 account on the trade! But with the stop-loss, if the stock starts tanking, you'd automatically sell at $99 a share, so you'd have $49,500 at the end of the day. Suppose it dropped to $75 a share. With the stop-loss order, it would have no impact on you. But if you didn't have the stop-loss order, you would have lost $12,500 on the trade.

Candles

When people day or swing trade, they use "technical analysis" in order to estimate future moves of the stock. The only difference between the two trading styles is the time frames over which the analysis is done. A day trader might be looking at 5-minute intervals to determine what trades to make over the next few hours, while a swing trader might be looking over the course of a few weeks for big swings in stock price.

One tool that is used in the analysis is candles. You can see candles on any stock chart by selecting them as a display option, and you can also set the time duration. Candles were actually invented by Japanese rice traders. Markets are universal.

The candles have "wicks" sticking out from them. These indicate the high and low prices for the time period. Candles are red or green in color. A red candle indicates selling off is dominant, while a green color indicates buying is dominant. Or put another way a red candle is associated with dropping stock prices, and green candles are associated with rising stock prices.

The top wick is the high share price for the period. The bottom wick is the low share price for the period. What the period depends on is what you select for the chart options. So, if you are looking at the chart with 5-minute intervals, the high and low prices indicate the high and low prices for each 5-minute interval.

The body is the solid block. If the block is green, then the top of the body is the closing price, and the bottom of the body is the opening price (price at the start of the time interval). For a red candle, it's the opposite, so the top is the opening price, and the bottom is the closing price. So, a red candle indicates the price dropped for the given time period; a green candle indicates the price rose over the given time period.

Traders use candles to estimate changes in the direction of the stock price. If a candle of one color engulfs the prior candle of the other color, which is its body is much larger in size, which can indicate a price reversal is coming. You can see it in the picture above, there is a red candle with a small body next to a green candle with a very large body, and that large green candle was followed by an increase in the share price. The large green body indicates that over that time interval, a large number of people bought shares of the stock, and increased demand means prices will be bid upwards.

A hammer is a candlestick with a small body and a long wick below it.

A green hammer at the bottom of a downtrend can indicate that stock prices are about to go higher. So that is a buy signal. If the hammer is upside down, it's called an inverted hammer or a shooting star, for a red candlestick. These occur at the tops of uptrends, and that indicates the stock price is about to begin dropping. A shooting star is a sell signal.

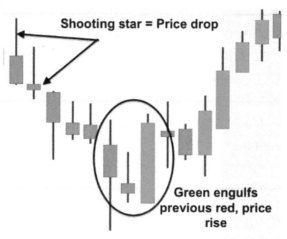

Day trading and swing trading are not for everyone, but they can be used to generate short term profits. Some people like the analysis and getting involved in the short term moves of the stock, so taking a very active role in trading. If the idea intrigues you, but day trading seems too risky, consider swing trading, which really isn't that risky in comparison, but you should always use stop-loss orders and be ready to take profits when they come rather than holding too long hoping to get more profits. Also, it's possible to mix things up, and you can put some of your capital into long term investments and use other capital to fund some level of swing or day trading. As we will see later, people interested in short term profits in the stock market can also use options trading.

CHAPTER 15:

How to Become a Successful Day Trader?

To be a successful day trader, you must have a goal in mind before investing.

Setting a Goal

Define what makes you want to get up and go to work every day. Want to go on vacation? Need to pay off student loans? Want a new car? Whatever the reason may be, defining a goal will help new traders be able to reach their potential.

A goal should always be measurable and have a timeframe attached to it. Measurable goals can help people see how far they have come, and timeframes allow for meeting deadlines and defining new goals.

An important thing to remember is that day trading is not a "get-rich-quick" scheme. Keeping goals realistic will help bring success.

Strategies

The next step after defining your goal is to strategize on how it's going to become a reality.

It is important to know some concepts that directly relate to your strategy. These concepts are the required capital and leverage.

Leverage

Day traders use either their own money (cash account) or by borrowing money from a broker (margin account).

This is an important decision to make. Trading with a cash account is often a safer option, but profits are limited to the amount of cash the trader has available.

Margin accounts are the most popular among day traders. With a margin account, traders can use the money provided by the broker to increase earnings per transaction, but they will also be increasing the amount they lose if the market turns for the worse.

Brokers also may ask for a deposit into the account before allowing a trader to use the platform.

Leverage is a straightforward concept with stocks. Let us say a trader buys $1000 of XYZ Inc. by putting up $500 and borrowing the other half of the money from the broker. The ending value after the trade is $1040. This would mean that the net equity will be $540, and the trader will have gotten an 8% return on the investment when the change in stock price was only 4%. So, the leverage allowed the trader to double his returns. However, this could have ultimately been double the loss as well.

How Much Should You Risk Per Trade?

In stock trading, a lot usually has 100 shares, and price increments are very small. Suppose a trader buys a lot at $20 per share and places the stop-loss at $19.50. In this case, the risk will be $0.50. For 100 shares, the total amount at risk will be $50.

Is this a suitable trade to make? Most traders recommend staying at or below the 1% mark as an accepted risk. Regardless of how good of an opportunity, a trader should keep 99% of the account balance intact.

Let us apply this logic to the above example. We are risking a total of $50 and our total account balance is $2000. By dividing $2000 by 1%, we get how much balance our account should have. The division gives us $20, which is 2.5x more than the amount of risk $50. So, the risk involved in making this trade is significantly higher than what we should risk per trade.

As per the risk strategy, to perform this trade, we need to have not less than $5000 in the account balance (which translates to $50 risk tolerance).

Stock Selection

Successful day traders always choose to trade stocks with the highest liquidity (traded at high volumes). One of the best things about choosing a liquid stock is that it can be easily bought and sold. This is since it has a large volume of shares that you can trade without having to worry about significant price changes.

In day trading, day traders must apply speed and precision in their strategies. Working with a high-volume stock will make it easier for day traders to enter and exit trades.

Day traders also need to consider the depth of the market (how many shares are available to trade). This will tell them how many shares they can buy from a certain corporation without causing significant price appreciation.

Day traders also choose stocks with medium to high volatility. Price movement is very important for day traders because this is where they can make money. Thus, choosing volatile stocks is important. Volatile stocks are those companies that are experiencing large price swings, resulting in a significant gap in their Intraday high points and low points.

Day trader chooses stocks that are group followers. What are group followers? Basically, these are stocks or equities that imitate the movements of their specific sector or index groups. How do you find these stocks? Simple. Just observe all those individual stock prices that increase when the index or sector goes upward.

Take note that if your strategy is trading the same stock every day, you do not have to mind if your stock is a group follower. The wisest thing you can do is to just focus your attention on that one stock.

Only pay attention to the current Intraday trend. If you have been around with other traders, you might have been given wise advice to "trade with the trend." The most experienced traders will advise to "trade with the trend because "the trend is the day trader best friend."

But of course, as a trader, you also have to accept that there is also an end to the trend... and when that time comes, you do have to part ways. But as long as the trend is there, you have to ride the waves. How do you do it? Well, keep it simple.

If you see that there is an uptrend, take long positions. As we said earlier, trends will not be there to stay, but you can make around one or two trades before the trend changes. If you are lucky, you can even make more.

But remember, once the dominant trend changes, go out and do not come back again till a new trend can be observed.

If you want to pick out the best stocks for Intraday trading, try to compare them with the S&P 500 or Nasdaq indexes. Ideally, look for stocks that have moderate to high correlation with these indexes. Now, what kind of stocks should you be trading during an uptrend?

The Entry Strategy

Always wait for the pullback, sometimes, traders become too impatient, especially during an upward trend that they decide to go on another route. But this should not be if you want to gain the best profits. Experts say that waiting for a pullback will give you lots of benefits. How will you go about this?

Start by looking at the trend lines so that you will have a rough estimate of where the price waves start and stop. You can use this when you are choosing stocks for trading to see if you can make an entry into the next price wave early on that will take you in the direction of the trend. If you are planning to buy a stock that you are expected to rise in value, buy it after you note a downward movement in the price and moves towards the higher point.

Always take profits regularly. As a trader, you do not really have a lot of time to capture profits, which is why it is very important that you do not spend a lot of time in trades that are not letting you make money. Also, make sure to avoid getting into trades that are not moving in the right direction.

When can you make profits? When the market is moving in an upward direction, you can take profits when the price matches or goes slightly above the price high in the current trend.

Stop-loss

Stop-loss is your safeguard. It is the stock price level, which, if reached, you will ask your broker to automatically exit the trade and sell the stocks you bought. This helps to limit your losses.

The determination of the level of the stop-loss is based on your risk tolerance and the technical analysis of the trend.

An important thing to understand here is the relation between your entry point and stop-loss. The stop-loss is not static, but once you enter the trade you can change your stop-loss, according to the behavior of the tread, but remember you must only change the stop-loss in the up direction, never set it below the level you specified when you chose your entry point.

The Exit Strategy

If there is an entry point to trading, there is also an exit point. If you have been trading for a while, you will know that entering a trade is quite easier than getting out of it. Exiting a trade is the part where you will know if you made a profit or you acquired losses.

The easiest way to close or exit a trade is to use a profit target. According to Investopedia, a profit target is a "predetermined point at which an investor will exit a trade in a profitable position." Say, for example, your profit target is $11.35. You bought the stock at $11.25 and sold it at $11.35. When the price reaches $11.35, you can go ahead and exit the trade.

Now, you have to take note that placing a profit target also needs to be balanced. Your main goal here is to earn the optimum profit potential, according to the market tendencies that you are trading in. If you get too greedy and put a high price, you might not reach your target. If you put it too close, you might not earn a lot of profit for your efforts. So, it is up to you to decide, based on your skills as a trader. One of the pros of using profit targets is that you already know the risks and rewards of the trade before you even place a trade.

Another positive aspect is that if you base your profit target on the objective analysis, it will help you avoid feeling different emotions in trading such as availability bias, loss aversion, and lottery syndrome. This is because you already know that your profit target is in a good place since it is based on the actual chart that is being analyzed.

One of the downsides of using profit targets is that it requires a lot of skills. You cannot put them randomly based on gut feeling. So, if you think you are not that skilled enough on this strategy, try to think of other ways, or better yet, make yourself more skillful.

Another downside is that there is always a possibility that your profit target will not be reached. This is not good because if you continue to place your profit targets too far, you will not be winning any trades. In the same way, if your profit target is placed too close, you will not earn any profit from taking risks.

Thankfully, there are a few methods in which you can may the most out of your profit targets.

CHAPTER 16:

Picking the Best Time to Trade

Whether you are a beginner trader or a professional, you need to start relying on consistency. This is going to make it easier for you to pick the right stocks to invest in and can help you figure out if you are going to make a profit or not. For example, a stock that has consistent ups and downs in the market will be much easier to invest in because you know when the high and the low points will occur. A stock that is really volatile and doesn't have a pattern at all can be hard to invest in because you never know where it will go from one day to the next. There are a few tips that you can follow to make picking the best time to trade an easier decision.

When you want to trade in stocks, the best time to do this is the first two hours after your chosen market has opened, and then in the last hours before closing. So, trading between 9:30 and 11:30 is a good time to begin. This time is very volatile, which can give you a lot of price changes and a lot of potentials to make profits. Then, you can also consider trading at three to four in the afternoon because some big movements can occur at these times as well. For traders who can't spend all day trading and who only have a few hours available, the morning session is the best option.

If you are looking to trade in futures, when the market opens is the best time to trade. Active futures have trading activity all of the time, so the best opportunities for this will often start earlier than when the stock market opens. Try to focus your energy on trading between 8:30 to 11:00. The official time for closing the futures market can vary, but you can also look at trading during the last hour as well.

During the week, the forex market is available for trading all day long. The most popular day trading pair that you may want to work with is EUR/USD. The time when the forex market is the most volatile is between six and five GMT. For a day trader who wants to work with the forex market, you should focus most of your energy on trading during that time. Often, the biggest changes in prices will occur from 12 PM to 3 PM GMT. This is when both the US and the London markets are open, which means that both groups are doing a lot of trading at the same time.

Despite the common belief about day trading, you don't have to spend all day on the computer doing your trades, unless you want to. This can be hard to keep up with and may end up leading you to a lot of anxiety and stress. Chances are, many traders are going to be more consistent and make more profits if you only spend a few hours trading in the market each day. Going with some of the times that we have listed above, depending on the market you want to trade in, can make a big difference.

Overall, you can earn a profit when you trade any time of the day as long as you have a good trading strategy and you know when to enter and when to exit the market. So, if there is some reason why you can't be available right at the beginning or right at the end of the market, then don't fret about it too much. You can always trade at the time that works best for you.

CHAPTER 17:

Options Trading

Options trading is not new to the game of finance. In fact, the practice has been around since before 332 BC, as its first record was mentioned in a book called Politics, published in 332 BC by Aristotle. This practice allowed people to purchase the right to buy an asset without actually buying the asset outright.

Aristotle introduced this topic by writing about a man called Thales of Miletus. Thales was a revered astronomer, philosopher, and mathematician in ancient Greece. His practice of options trading started when he used the stars and weather patterns to predict that a huge olive harvest would come in the following year. With the first prediction, he then stated that olive presses would be in high demand to facilitate such a huge harvest. Forward-thinker that he was, Thales understood that he could turn a huge profit if he was the one to own all of the olive presses in the region.

While he did not have the kind of money that allowed him to buy all of the olive presses outright, he did use the small amount that he did have to secure the use of all olive presses in that region by using the olive presses themselves as the underlying asset to facilitate the transaction.

His prediction came true and the olive harvest was plentiful. As the one who had the option to all the olive presses in the region, Thales had the option to use them himself during harvest time (exercising the option) or sell them to other people who would pay more for the same right that he owned at the time (selling the options to earn a profit). He chose to sell the right to use the olive presses to harvesters and thus, turned a huge profit.

Options trading found its way into modern trading practices as it moved into European classic economics and finance in 1636. Due to unregulated practices, options trading got a bad reputation. However, this did not stop investors from acknowledging that trading options allowed them to gain powerful leverage in the finance arena.

Options trading was brought into the United States in 1872 by an American financier called Russell Sage. By using options trading, Sage was able to accumulate millions of dollars in just a few years, even though the practice of trading options was illiquid and unstandardized during that time. He even bought a seat in the NYSE in 1874. Unfortunately, Sage lost a small fortune during the stock market crash of 1884 and gave up trading options. Other traders and investors saw the potential that options trading had, though, and continued the practice.

It took about 100 years, but options trading became standardized and regulated by the government as it gained increasing popularity, and more advances were made in defining how the public traded options. I am ever grateful that the practice stood the test of time and became an integral part of modern stock marketing investing.

My start on the stock market came with options trading. Options trading allowed me to enter the stock market back when I did not have the finances to buy and sell stock outright. Even though the learning curb was sharp, especially since information was not as readily available back when I just started, the benefits allowed me to accumulate enough wealth so that I could turn to investing in pricier forms of trading on the stock market like buying and selling stocks, mutual funds and exchange-traded funds.

Even though the affordability was great, it was the no obligation nature of this form of trading that pulled me in the hardest back then. By utilizing options trading, I was under no legal commitment to buy or sell anything unless it was advantageous for me to do so. As a man who did not have as many assets signed to his name back when I just started as a trader, this was great because the risks were significantly lower compared to the act of outright buying and selling of stocks.

Because of the powerful leverage trading options allows me, I still use this trading practice today as a way to keep my portfolio balanced and to enter markets, I am unsure about but want to test for profitability. The best part is that getting started with options trading is not all that different than getting started with buying and selling stocks. Ensure that this practice is incorporated into your trading plan, that you have the necessary accounts and representation through a brokerage firm, get your feet wet with paper trading and then choose your trading style, then you will be all set to start trading options! Day trading is the full-time practice of stock market trading and positions trading. It is the stock market trading style most commonly used by professionals. It is also the style most used for options trading.

What are Options?

Stocks and options are two items that are often mistakenly thought to be the same, but they are not the same thing. Stocks are a typical component of options. Options are a great way of investing in the stock market without outright buying stock or any other security. This method of investing allows investors to invest in the stock market with a lower amount while still having the potential to earn the same profit that a stocks trader would.

Options are financial contracts that derived their value from the securities attached to them. The contract states that the holder of the option has the right (option) to buy or sell the security on or by a date specified at a specific price. This specified date is called the expiration date. The name option comes from the fact that there is no obligation for the holder of the contract to take any particular course of action.

The options that the option holder has include:

- Sell the option to another investor.
- Exercise the contract and buy the asset.
- Exercise the option and sell all or part of the asset.
- Allow the option to expire without following any particular course of action.

The specific selling or buying price that the option can be exercised for is called the strike price. This price does not change, no matter what happens after the date of signing.

Instead of buying or selling the security, investors of options pay a premium to the seller of the option. Options premium pricing is a complex process because there are so many factors that go into developing each one. It would be a simple process if the premium was just based on the value of the stock or other securities, but it is not. And there is not going around the process either because premium pricing needs to be fair to all the parties involved in the transaction.

The intrinsic value of the security also factors into the development of the option premium. This value is determined by finding the difference between the current market price of the security and the strike price of the option.

The time value is also another factor that makes up the premium of an option. Time value is the amount an investor would willingly pay in addition to the premium because there is the underlying belief that the security value will rise in the future.

Other factors that affect the creation of options premium include:

- Volatility
- Interest rates
- Dividends

Luckily, there are pricing models that help with the creation of option premiums so it does not have to be calculated manually.

CHAPTER 18:

Position Trading

Position trading is when you hang on to a stock for several weeks or even months. Position traders hang on for a longer period than swing traders. You are more focused on a longer-term game plan and you're confident that the gains that you would accomplish with such a longer timeline are going to be higher than if you tried other strategies. The biggest factors for position trading involve three elements: news trends, earnings cycle, and industry trends.

News Trends

Traders who use a position trading strategy essentially invest in the stock. The fact that they're digging in for up to several months shows that they're investing in the value of the stock being appreciated by the broader market.

One of the main factors that they base this strategy on is the news involving the particular stock. Maybe there's some sort of drug application approval that's spending. Maybe there's some sort of a new patent or program that was launched. Whatever the case may be, there is an event that was made known to the public, and there is some sort of a cut off in the future regarding a decision on that event.

For example, a biotechnology company may have been developing a breakthrough cancer drug for several years. All that time, the stock may have been going up and down or trading sideways. A position trader would take a position on that stock if there was news that within a few weeks or a few months, there would be an FDA decision regarding its drug application.

Now, what makes many biotechnology stocks fairly good position plays is the fact that they are fairly predictable in terms of their news cycles. In the United States, for new medication to be approved by the FDA, there have to be some several phases in the drug application. There are the lab trials, the clinical trials, and the formal application. Each of these news events can be points in time where the position trader can buy into the company.

Using the biotechnology example once again, if a company is working on an anti-cancer drug, they would first announce that their lab results indicate that they have a promising compound. When the news comes out, this can be a buying opportunity. However, it's anybody's guess whether this seemingly promising technology would really pan out, as far as commercialization is concerned, because the drug still has to go from internal laboratory testing to wider lab testing, to human clinical trials, and then formal application.

A position trader can take a position on the stock and wait until the next phase comes. Usually, they would wait until that point in time where clinical trials look so promising that the company can then file a formal application. The stock can move quite a bit once a formal application is tendered by the company.

Can you imagine the effect on the stock when the FDA finally approves the application? So, the key point here is there are fairly well-defined milestones for a biotechnology company's proposed drug to get approved. Position traders can look at the milestones and take positions accordingly. It's not uncommon for traders who specialize in biotechnology stocks to enter and leave a biotech stock several times as the company moves closer and closer to drug approval.

Other news trends to look out for involve strategic partnerships. For example, a company has just partnered with a large retail or pharmaceutical chain spread throughout the United States. Such deals and business developments can have a very positive material impact on a company's sales figures.

The position trader would then look at the announcement and then buy into the company based on the projected timeline of when the results of that static partnership will be released. Depending on how big the deal is, the position trader can actually make quite a bit of money if the distribution deal of the business alliance has a fairly significant impact on the company's bottom line.

Earnings Cycle

Another fairly predictable milestone or series of events position traders take advantage of our earnings cycles.

When a company is about to announce its earnings in a month, a position trader would look at recent news releases to see if there is a positive trend here, or if there is a negative trend. Either way, the position trader would take up a position.

In the case of a positive trend, the position trader would buy long. In terms of negative trends, the trader would sell short. Whatever the case may be, there is a fairly short and predictable period of time between the time the trader took up a position and when the earnings event comes. Either the company made more money or made less money, the event will come, and the position trader can then liquidate his or her position.

It's important to note that there's a little bit of complication. Wall Street has evolved to the point that if a company manages to meet expectations, that may not be enough in of itself to boost the company's stock. In many cases, Wall Street expects companies to beat street expectations to gain a nice boost up.

For example, if Facebook announced that they are going to be making a dollar share and Facebook comes in at exactly a dollar share, chances are that performance was already factored into the stock price of Facebook by the time its next earnings cycle milestone comes up.

Now, compare this with Facebook announcing that it made a $1.25 profit per share. Assuming that the consensus expectation was $1 per share, this makes for tremendous news. A position trader that bought before the earnings cycle stands to gain a lot of money due to the fact that the company beat expectations. Always factor in the power of street expectations when it comes to the earnings cycle.

Don't be surprised if you take a long position several weeks before the earnings cycle plays out, and only for your stock to remain the same price or to even decline. Pay attention to street expectations. It is not uncommon for stocks to hit their announced earnings target and still see their stock price sink. Why? Wall Street was expecting the company to beat expectations. Simply coming in to meet expectations is not enough.

If you think that's bad, it's especially worse if the company misses expectations. If, for example, Amazon stock was expected to earn a dollar per share, but the actual figure is 90 cents per share, this can put a tremendous downward pressure on the stock. Always factor in expectations.

Industry Trends

Another big factor in position trading involves industry trends. If you noticed that an industry, as a whole, is poised for a breakout, then you can take a position in leading companies in that industry. It all depends on whether this industry breakout or recovery is factored into the prices of the stock price of the biggest companies in that industry.

The key to playing industry trends is not to buy the giant players in that industry. Chances are whatever appreciation you get would be quite incremental because everybody's paying attention to those companies. A lot of people are playing those companies. Whatever upward movement in your positions may be would basically be diluted by the huge number of people buying and selling that stock.

Instead, look for mid-tier companies that have a track record of appreciating quite well during industry recoveries. Alternatively, you can take positions in growth stocks within that industry. The reason why you should pursue this strategy is that the weight of return to your position would probably be much higher compared to you betting on the biggest players in that industry you're tracking.

You have to understand the biggest players in any industry are usually already bought into by big mutual funds and pension funds. In short, their institutional coverage is very high, so they really have to outperform the industry tremendously for their stocks to get a nice lift up. This is not the case with middle tier or up and coming companies within that industry. These companies' stock prices can benefit tremendously if there is any sort of positive industry trend.

Risks in Position Trading

The biggest risk that you undertake when doing position trading doesn't involve your stock going down. Okay, let's just get that out of the way. Even if your stock were to tank, you should have a stop limit order on your stocks. Meaning, you decide for yourself going in what is the most you can afford to lose. You then put a stop limit sell order on that price.

For example, you buy into a stock that's worth $20. You then arrive at 10% as the maximum you're willing to lose on that position. Accordingly, if the stock ever dips down to $18, you will automatically neutralize your position. You will liquidate. You are completely out of the stock. This is how you protect yourself from your long position going south.

Believe me, this happens quite a bit. It doesn't happen all the time, but it does happen, so you need to protect yourself. At least you only lost at least 10%. You can then play the market again to recover. Also, keep in mind that when you lose money in stock trades, you can use that loss as an offset regarding any gains in the future. Still, the biggest worry you'll have when using a position trading strategy to stocks is that the stocks really don't go anywhere.

If you think about it, it may actually even be a good thing if the stock just sinks. Because once it sinks, you have set up your stop-limit order so that you are out of that stock. It just didn't pan out. The worst thing that can happen is for the stock to essentially track sideways. For example, if you buy a company that is worth $20 share and for the whole year, you took a position and the price of the company basically went from $20 to $19 to $21, and never really varied. Why is this a problem?

Well, the problem here is your money is not growing so you're not beating inflation. Second, you're paying a huge amount of money in the form of opportunity costs. Can you imagine if you were to have not invested in that stock in the first place and traded another stock that is volatile enough for you to lock in a sizable profit? Which position would you rather be in?

You better believe that the opportunity cost in position trading can be quite huge. This is why a lot of position traders diversify their long positions. They know that out of a basket of stocks, some would sink so they would immediately liquidate their position.

Always pay attention to the turnover of your capital because the timeframe might be so long that it turns out that it was really not worth your time and energy to have gotten into that stock at all. While the stock might appreciate a couple of percentage here and there, you're looking for a fairly substantial return to fully recoup and make up for whatever opportunity costs you suffered.

This is the key to position trading. Make sure that the gain you got compensates or more than compensates for the amount of time you waited for the stock to appreciate.

CHAPTER 19

Scalping

Traders can be divided into three types: swing traders, day traders, and scalpers. The three methods can be integrated, which is my preferred mode of operation.

Scalping refers to very short-term trades. Swing traders hold stocks over to the next day, and day traders generally try to get as much from the stock as possible within one day of trading. Both swing and day traders generally base their systems on technical analysis with a touch of fundamental analysis.

Scalpers are based one hundred percent on technical analysis. Their goal is the very short term. Changes of just a few cents for several seconds up to some minutes are sufficient. This means that in order to earn a livelihood from the market, scalpers need to trade in relatively larger amounts than day or swing traders. Scalpers with little backing (which is, sadly, the case for most of them) make up for what their pocket lacks by trading in financial products, which can be leveraged more than the typical leverage of the world of stock trading. These may include futures, leveraged twenty times more, options, and of course, FOREX (foreign exchange), which can reach leveraging of up to 500 times more, expressed as 500:1 margin. The absurdity is that trading in these strongly-leveraged products is harder and incredibly riskier than stock trading. Nonetheless, the dream of "striking it rich quick" draws people with no funds and no experience into the hardest areas of trading, where they will often begin, and almost invariably end, their trading careers.

Scalping Techniques

The first condition: you need to keep your finger on the mouse, and your eyes glued to the screen. You need to give your full attention to the stock. You must buy and sell with precise LIMIT orders.

You must absolutely NOT chase the stock, because, with scalping, profit or loss is measured in just a few cents. In many cases, I place an exit order in advance.

For example: if I buy 3000 shares at $20 and anticipate an increase of 30 cents, I will set a sell limit order in my trading platform of:

- 1000 shares at 20.15

- 1000 shares at 20.25

- And wait with my finger on the mouse for the first sign of weakness in order to sell the remaining 1000 shares

Smart Money

Scalps are meant to be short term and are therefore not executed in small quantities. Trading in small quantities of shares causes the "small-money syndrome" and leads to failure.

Scalping is not executed in small quantities of shares. New traders scalping in small quantities, such as 300 shares, find themselves caught in the trap of negligible profits, or as the phenomenon is known, the "small-money syndrome." Selling 100 shares for a profit of 15 cents seems like too small a yield, so they will try to drag the trade out for a few more cents, and usually discover that they have waited too long before selling. The stock pulls back down by 10 cents, so it does not pay to sell because the profit is even less now, and they wait a bit longer. Then the stock returns to their entry point, or even below it, and the scalping ends in a loss!

With large quantities of shares, by contrast, a decent profit is earned with each partial trade locked in, without the need to cope with the small-money syndrome.

The One-Cent Scalp

Cent scalping is a trading method geared at making profits of one or just a few cents, from light intraday fluctuations in stocks with "locked prices." Stocks with locked prices are stocks in which hundreds, if not thousands of traders, are operating, executing bids and asks at one cent above or below the stock's traded price. This is not a classic trading method based on noticeable intraday fluctuations resulting from breakouts, breakdowns, or direction changes. In contrast with everything we have learned so far, scalping for one cent is based chiefly on lack of volatility.

One Cent Scalping and the Commission Barrier

The first condition for participating in this method is to have a large trading account. If you want to profit from the movement of one cent and still overcome the barrier of commission, you need to operate with no less than 10,000 shares. A profit of one cent on 10,000 shares is worth $100, from which commission must still be deducted. The commissions with this method are the key to success or failure.

Here is an example: let us say that you profited one cent on 10,000 shares, producing $100. Let's assume that you pay a commission of one cent per share, and you bought 10,000 shares. That totals $100 profit, canceled out by the commission, and when you sell, that costs another $100. Altogether, a loss of $100. Even if you paid commission of one-tenth of a cent, totaling $20 for both buy and sell executions, you have still left 20% of your profit with the broker.

This may sound reasonable to you, but you must also take into account the sad fact that when you lose (at least 30% of your executions will end up as losses), the loss plus the commission will total $120. The weighted average is definitely to your detriment.

The solution: unlike the method of charging one cent per share, which will only be worthwhile if you operate in quantities of up to 2000 shares per click, when you trade in large fixed amounts, you need to ask your broker to define a different commission system based on the Per Trade Commission Plan rather than the Per Share Commission Plan. If you trade in large amounts, it is probable that you will be able to close on a price of $3 to $6 per click of the button, unlimited in quantity.

Large-scale traders usually receive commissions rather than pay them. How? When you set your bid and ask orders and wait for their execution, you are adding liquidity to the market! When you do that, as we have already learned, you receive a commission of $2 per 1000 shares from the ECN. With a simple calculation, you can understand that the relatively small quantity of 10,000 shares will bring you an ECN return of 0.2 cents per share, which is $20, while you paid only $6. What would happen with a quantity of 100,000 shares? The ECN return is worth $200, while the commission you pay is still $6. Can you see where this is going? I am familiar with traders who make their living from buying and selling a share at exactly the same price, for profits of hundreds of dollars from the ECN return alone. If they're lucky, they also manage to earn another cent per share.

Sound easy? No, it isn't easy at all!

One-Cent Scalping: The Method First find a low-priced stock

This should ideally be in the $5 to $10 range, with low volatility and a volume of tens of millions of shares per day.

The candidates change during different periods of market activity, volatility, and price. Remember that volatility is this method's worst enemy. Just imagine how much you could lose if the stock moved ten cents against you! This is also why you MUST operate according to the following rules:

1. The stock must be moving sideways with no trend, or in industry terms, the stock must have a locked price.

2. The stock must show no volatility and movement of up to 5-10 cents per day

3. The market is moving sideways with no trend (generally occurs during lunch hours)

4. The stock is priced up to $10. You can buy cheap stocks in large quantities even if your name is not Warren Buffet

5. The stock shows large trading volume of tens of millions per day

The simplest way to choose a stock is to fish it out of the list that always contains the "top ten" high volume stocks traded on NASDAQ or NYSE. Notice that I do not relate to stocks that made it into the list by chance, but those who are on that listing constantly. On some days, you might choose Bank of America (BAC) or Intel (INTC), Microsoft (MSFT) or others. Citigroup (C) used to be the scalpers' favorite as long as its price hovered around the $4 mark in volumes of hundreds of millions of shares per day before the reverse split was executed, as already described.

When you bring these stocks up on your screen, you will see intraday volumes of tens, if not hundreds of millions of shares, and enormous numbers of bidders and askers. Many of them are playing the one-cent game.

Who, in fact, shifts the stock if no one wants it to move more than one cent? Of course, this would not be the scalpers working at the single cent level, because they are basically locking the price and preventing movement. The real change comes from the public and from funds bidding and asking with long-term investment in mind, and they are not interested in whether the stock has gone up or down one-cent.

Let's assume you have chosen your stock and it's time to trade. The operation itself is fairly simple but requires a good deal of experience. First, even if the price is moving sideways, examine the overall market trend and the stock's trend. If the trend is up, you will want to execute a long rather than a short, and vice versa. Now you need to enter your buy limit order in the BID, and wait patiently until sellers hit your bid. The moment you have bought the desired quantity, you enter a sell limit order on the ASK side, with a profit target of 1 to 3 cents, and wait for buyers to hit your ask in the reverse direction.

Notice that there is no need to use the short order since for most of the trading platforms, the regular SELL will operate exactly like a short. Now that you have sold the quantity you bought at a profit, and added to that sale a double quantity, you are in a short and therefore need to position a double quantity on the BID side with a targeted profit of 1 to 3 cents, repeating the cycle. Once the market becomes more volatile, and based on the premise that you are on the right side of market direction, you need to cancel the exit order and try to profit from a few more cents beyond the original profit target.

I wish to stress, yet again, that this method sounds simple. In reality, it requires a great deal of patience, self-discipline, and deep familiarity with the market. You need to follow the stock chart in one-minute candles. You also need to watch the market chart, which will indicate if you need to flee the trade with an unexpected loss, or cancel an exit order and let the market take you to unanticipated profits of a few additional cents.

CHAPTER 20:

Value Investing

Value investing or fundamental investing is also known as the Warren Buffett School of Investing. Warren Buffett is a world-famous investor. He lives in Omaha, Nebraska, and this man is responsible for growing his investors' money several thousand times. I'm not saying that his stocks are worth several thousand dollars, I'm talking several thousand percent appreciations. That's how awesome of an investor Warren Buffet is.

The interesting thing about his investing style is he really doesn't pay attention to what the current price of the company is. Instead, he looks at long term value. It may well turn out that the stock of a company seems fairly high by today's standards. However, to Buffett, the stock is actually cheap in light of its future value.

The secret to value investing is the future value. You basically would have to look at the track record of the company, its current operations and health, as well as the health of the industry it's in. You then project this information in the future factoring in potential future conditions. Once you have a fairly clear picture, you then buy in, and it's important to note that you basically don't leave. That's the whole point of value investing.

You buy and you hold. You're playing the long game. This strategy is strictly for people who buy long. You might be asking yourself, well, if I buy long then I might be suffering opportunity cost because I could have been making more money in the short term buying a more volatile stock?

Believe me, if you play the biotech or internet stocks, they can be quite volatile. It's not uncommon for traders to make thousands of dollars every single day of volatility of these stocks. They move that quickly. Warren Buffett doesn't care about any of that. Instead, his game is to basically hold the company for several years or even decades and at the end of that long period, the stock has split many times or has gone up in value so much.

If you ever need proof of this, look at his main investment vehicle, Berkshire Hathaway. Can you imagine if you have bought Berkshire Hathaway in the 80s? You would be a millionaire many times over today. That's how awesome of an investor Warren Buffet is. He's all about the long game. He's all about patient investing.

Now, value investing may not fit your investment goals. If your immediate goal is to have your money appreciate by 10% or 15% per year, value investing may not be a slam dunk. You have to understand that value investing looks at growth over time. It may be substantial growth. We're talking about the company's stock price doubling or even tripling, but it's anybody's guess when this will exactly happen.

It's not uncommon for a stock to only appreciate 5% the next year, and then the year after that goes up to 20%, and then dips down to 10%, so on and so forth. But when you average everything out, it turns out that the stock has actually doubled, tripled, or even quadrupled in price.

How to do Value Investing

Warren Buffett is known for simply reading the financial statements of a company, as well as their financial papers in the comfort of his office. He would then make phone calls to make million-dollar stock purchases. That's all he does. He usually never goes to the actual company. He usually never reads the paper or checks out the news regarding the company.

All he pays attention to are their numbers. I don't expect you to master the game so well that you only need to see numbers. This is why you need to pay attention to the following factors.

Focus on CASH FLOW

Solid companies have cash flow volumes that justify their price. The company must be generating revenue. Even if it is no earning a profit, it must have enough cash flow to justify its price either now or at some point in the future. Depending on how speculative the stock is, cash flow is determined by either P/E or price-to-book.

(P/E) Price to Earnings Ratio: The company's earnings per share is cross-referenced to its current stock price. For example: if a company is earning $1 per share is trading at $20 per share, its P/E ratio is 20. This is an indication of cash flow value in reference to its current price. If you're going to use P/E as your cash flow factor, you should compare different stocks that have the same fundamentals (industry positioning, book value, growth factors, and others).

Price to book Ratio: After reading a company's balance sheet, you will be aware of all the assets a company has. After proper depreciation and discounting, whatever amount left is the liquidation value of the company's assets. In other words, if you were going to liquidate the company and get cash for all assets and you take out whatever debt the company owes, what's left is its book value. Price to book is the ratio of how many times the company's book value is multiplied to produce its current per share value. For example: if you have a company that has a book value of $10 per share and it trades for $100 per share, the price to book value is 10.

Please note that there are many other cash flow-based value calculation methods, but P/E and price to book are the most common and are enough to guide any beginner investor. As you become more proficient at trading, you might want to scale up using other methods at calculating cash flow.

Focus on Industry Leaders

The first thing you need to do is to look for industry leaders or potential leaders in an industry. It's important to look at solid companies. These companies are doing something right. They're making money.

They have made an impact. They've got their act together. It's important to focus on these qualities.

The problem with a lot of stock out there is that a lot of them are sold based on hype and potential. For example, Twitter traded as high as the low 40s because people are optimistic that somehow, someway, it's going to make money. Its valuation wasn't really based on how the company was run, how much money it was making, its position in the industry. None of that matter. All the focus was on potential growth.

Not so with value investing. You look at the actual position of the company and the fact that it is already making money. You start with that fact. The company has to be already well-positioned. This doesn't mean that the company has already dominated its industry or is the number one player. It can be an up and comer. What's important is that it has the house in order.

It must have Solid Financials

A key indicator that a company has its financial house in order is that it has zero to low debt. A company that has almost no debt and a low stock price is actually quite underpriced. This is the kind of combination that Warren Buffett gets excited about. He knows that chances are quite good that for some reason or another, the market simply is not acknowledging the solid fundamentals of a company. And one key factor in that is its debt exposure.

If the company has almost zero debt and a low stock price and a solid market or industry presence, then the company has a good chance of being a good value investment. However, you need to look at other factors as well.

The Company is in a Growing Industry

Now, can you imagine doing your research in stocks and finding a company that is a soon to be an industry leader, or is already an industry leader and has zero debt? It is also very profitable currently. On top of all of this, its stock is fairly low, as measured by price per earnings ratio (P/E). Sounds like a slam dunk, right?

Well, hold your horses. Pay attention to the company that industry is in. It may well turn out that that company is the only gem in that industry because that industry is basically going downhill. In that situation, that company is probably going to have a bleak future. Its stock price might look good now, but it's only a matter of time until that company implodes or has to reinvent itself and enter another industry.

Pay attention to the industry. Is it under a tremendous amount of disruption? Or is it still a growing industry? The problem with industries that are under a tremendous amount of disruption is that you really don't know the direction the industry would go.

For example, the Eastman Kodak Corporation was the top dog of the photographic materials industry. Thanks to the rise of digital cameras, the photographic material industry is a shadow of its former self. It still exists in a very limited form, but it's definitely not big enough to sustain a company that's as gigantic as the Eastman Kodak.

Do you see how this works? And the problem was that the industry that was under serious disruption during the 90s and early 2000s. Steer clear from companies that are under disruption because it's anybody's guess what the ultimate direction of the technology or business strategies of the companies in that industry.

Heavy Cash Flow and large Cash Position

Another factor value investor looks at is how much cash a company has on its book. Now, this is the key indicator of how well that company is run. If a company is profitable but it essentially just burns up its remaining cash on research and development, the company might not be a solid value investment because it's essentially spending a lot of money to make a lot of money.

Ultimately, it's basically just trying to tread water. This is not always the case. It also depends on the industry. Still, if you notice that a company has a lot of cash in its balance sheet and almost zero debt, that company is doing something right and if you can see that the cash at hand is growing over time, then this is a key indicator that this company may be a solid value investment, with everything else being equal.

Pay attention to accounts receivable. While a healthy level of accounts receivables is fine, a company that has an extremely high A/R level merits further and deeper analysis. It might be having a tough time collecting and you need to be very careful about how they log these. The company might only seem like it is worth a lot of money.

"Underappreciated Stocks"

Warren Buffett makes a big deal about underappreciated stocks. In fact, in many of his interviews, he talks about buying stocks that are underappreciated. Now, a lot of people would define "underappreciated stocks" as companies whose stock prices are a bargain compared to other companies in the Dow Jones Industrial Average.

This is a misconception. A stock is underappreciated, in classical value investment terms, not based on how it compares to other companies but based on its potential future value.

CHAPTER 21:

Dividend Investing

What is Dividend Investing?

Dividend Investing is a term describing an approach in investment, which entails purchasing stocks that have dividends. The main goal of Dividend investing is the generation of a stable passive income. Dividend investing is not as simple as its definition. There are intricacies involved.

For those that are not in the finance field, this may make the reading of the book a little bit difficult to understand. However, here are some terms you should look out for in the course of reading. Knowing these terms should help simply their use as we move forward.

Stock: This term refers to a kind of security that equates proportionate ownership in the issuer company. Alternatively, a stock is called shares.

Dividend: This term is simply the portion of a company's profit paid to its shareholders. Dividends are not necessarily cash. They are in shares and other properties.

If you are not well convinced about dividend investing, it is time you stopped doubting the potentials of this investment strategy. There are many benefits of dividend investing, but the accessible advantage that everyone will derive from is that it is an ideal source of retirement income. When you retire, you have the privilege to take some of your dividend payments and still retain ownership of stocks, which will continually pay you for the rest of your life.

Why Invest in Dividend Stocks?

Notwithstanding the economic importance of dividend stocks, there are articles, books, and even experts' comments that discredit Dividend investing. As a result, many people are left undecided about the decision to invest in dividend stocks. "What if the company slashes the price of their dividends abruptly?"

"I read it up an article that the payment of dividends does not determine shares prices." These comments are some of the reasons why specific individuals are left undecided about the decision to invest in dividend stocks. Undoubtedly, nothing in this world has no pros and cons. The same principle applies to investment in dividend stocks. The good news about investing in dividend stocks is that the advantages greatly outweigh the cons.

Besides, the few drawbacks of investing in dividend stocks should not make you lose a chance of a steady income. As an investor, if you want to make it financially, you must be willing to take a risk. Even if you choose not to invest in a dividend stock, there is a risk in your decision. You risk the chance of not benefiting from the earnings of dividend stocks.

Despite the few limitations of dividend stocks, there are countless reasons why you should invest in dividend stocks. So, to the big question:

What Are the Benefits of Investing in Dividend Stocks?

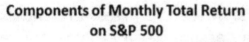

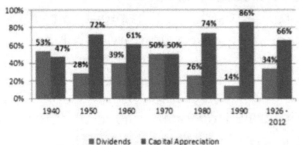

Source: Dow Jones S&P Indices LLC

Image showing the rate at which dividend investing can multiply your returns over time.

Dividend Stocks Investment Is an Avenue to Secure a Stable Stream of Income

One merit of dividend stock over other types of stocks is that it helps you achieve a source of passive income that is both steady and reliable. Unlike other forms of investments, you don't have to sell anything to make a profit.

When you invest in other types of stocks, you tend not to make a profit until you sell them. The set back of this characteristic is that you merely have a paper profit until you sell something. Yes, you make a profit. But the gain is only on paper as you are unable to cash out your rewards and earnings till you sell something. So, most investments are not ideal for a steady passive income.

The situation is different when you invest in dividend stocks. The primary thing that distinct dividend stocks from other investment options are that there are no paper profits. When you invest in Dividend investing, you have the assurance of cashing out raw and cold cash. There is no strict requirement to tell your broker to sell something when you are involved in Dividend investing.

Dividends are your earned money. Once paid, they cannot withdraw from you; this is the best part about investing in dividend stocks.

Also, the norm is that companies pay dividends frequently of a fiscal quarter (that is, every three months). If you are an investor seeking to multiply his/her income; dividend stocks, this is an investment option that you should consider. There is a guarantee for you to earn payment every three months. Say goodbye to financial inadequacy.

Investment in Dividend Stocks Translates to a Sufficient Income in the Retirement Period

When you invest in dividend stock for the long term, you're privileged to have a stable income when you retire. Here is a reason why you should invest in dividend stocks, and do so as soon as possible.

Research by several finance professionals shows that investors who build a dividend stock portfolio for the long term are more likely to acquire many shares when they age. The implication of having many Dividend-paying stocks at an old age or retirement period is that you have more than enough money to cater to your financial problems.

You should invest in dividend-paying stocks because they are futuristic than their counterparts. When you buy dividend-paying stocks, you are confident in your decision, as you know that you are making a financial decision that guarantees financial freedom. Investing in dividend stocks brings you both short-term and long-term rewards.

For instance, a nurse named Jane makes steps towards securing her financial future by investing in dividend stocks by the time she is 40. If her dividend income is $50 at the time, with time, the income grows to $100 and continuously adds up. By the time she is 60, Jane's dividend income would have added up to $20,000 that rolls in equity. So, if you want to be like Jane, or even better, invest in dividend stocks.

Investment in Dividend Stocks Grants You the Privilege to Retain Your Shares and Ownership at the Same Time

Dividend stocks are not like other investment options. Typically, if you invest in a stock that does not pay a dividend, the only way for you to make money out of your shares is by selling them out. The implication of this is that you cannot make a profit and retain ownership of your shares. With ordinary shares, you cannot earn a profit while maintaining your stocks; you have to give in something for something, vis-à-vis.

The fear of losing ownership to gain profit is what pushes many people away from investing. They are incredibly skeptical of any form of investment due to their generalization of stocks. Not all stocks are the same. Dividend stocks, for instance, is significantly different from other types of stocks that do not pay dividends. Naturally, as humans, we are selfish, and we don't love losing out. Thus, we always want to gain. We don't accommodate the fear of making a loss; this is why some investors do not like the idea of selling shares. They are of the notion that selling their stocks in a company will affect them, especially in periods where growth is probable. So, people tend to reject the idea of investing in stocks as they believe earning profit makes them lose their source of income and ownership in a company.

As earlier stated, all stocks are not the same. The shares which prevent dual privilege of ownership and profitability are those that do not pay in dividends. Dividends paying stocks permits you to make money off your shares while still being in control of them. If you invest in dividend stocks, you do not have to fear the relinquishment of your ownership in a company.

With an investment in dividend stocks, you make a profit off your stocks while owning them for the possibility of capital appreciation.

Inflation Has Almost Nothing on Dividend Stocks

During inflation periods, your earnings are affected negatively. Despite the negative effect of inflation, you can keep your passive income safe from the negative impact that inflation hampers on the economy. When you invest in dividends paying stocks, you can WIN (Whip Inflation Now).

If you are a follower of history, then you are likely to remember that the WIN word came about in President Gerald Ford's administration. If you are ignorant about what happened, here is a quick recap. Back in August 1974, President Ford charged Americans to Whip Inflation Now (WIN) as there was a growing rate of inflation in the country then (about 11%). And the WIN strategy proved useful for most Americans as it provided a hedge against inflation.

Investment in dividend stocks protects your investment earnings from inflation; thus, if you are looking forward to ample protection in inflation periods. If you want to smile while others are crying wolf, invest in dividend stocks.

A significant benefit of dividends over most income-generating investments is that they can keep pace with the rate of inflation. Dividend stock prices increase as the general price level in an economy increases. When prices inflate, companies gain more profit. The increased earnings of companies permit them to increase the rates of dividend payments. Consequently, you make more profit as an investor. However, inflation still takes a bite out of your investment income as a modest 3% inflation has the potential to reduce the 7% on your annual earnings to a meager sum of 4%.

Investing in Dividend Stocks Provides a Win-Win Opportunity

Most investment generating options do not allow you to win totally. For instance, you are an investor solely in ordinary shares that do not pay in dividends; you are likely to succeed in only one way. The only way that you can win is if you sell the stock at a high price. Ironically, you suffer a more significant loss as instability is almost synonymous with Wall Street (stock exchange market). There is no surety that share prices will increase to an amount that earns you profit. Even if a while is stable, the stability is often short-lived due to frequent fluctuations of shares value. Therefore, there is a probability that you may lose in two ways when you invest in ordinary shares. You drop in profitability at regular intervals, and more importantly, you lose the ownership of your stocks.

The situation of things is a little bit better when you invest in dividend stocks. While you are subject to the same culture of the instability of Wall Street, you are more secure when you invest in dividends stocks. Unlike other types of shares, dividends provide the win-win option. You have considerably stable ownership of your stocks while making money from it in your possession. If the issuing corporation pays you your dividend check and your stock value increase at the same time, you make terrific money from income and capital appreciation. If you don't want to earn your dividend immediately, you can reinvest it to buy more stocks.

As earlier stated, Wall Street is not all bed of roses. You can equally lose out when you invest in dividend stocks. Investing in dividend stocks does not give you immunity from frequent loss. But you are safer than when you rely only on shares that do not reward in dividends.

CHAPTER 22:

Growth Investing

Growth investing is often contrasted with value investing as being a completely different style of making money in the markets. The truth is that both approaches overlap with one another. This is going to give you a good introduction to growth investing, as well as clarify how you can capture growth profitably and with as little risk as possible in your portfolio.

Definition

So, what is growth investing anyway, and why is it a good strategy to follow? As the name suggests, the idea here is to capture the growth inherent in a company. The aim is to identify companies that have huge growth prospects for the future and have the earnings and competitive edge to back this up. The focus of growth investing is to capture capital gains.

This is because companies that are growing fast need all the cash, they can get their hands on. Therefore, paying dividends might not be the best option. Thus, investors who place their money in growth stocks are banking on the stock price rising enough so as to make them enough gains in the long run. This sounds like a risky strategy, but it's actually what proper investing is all about.

After all, the aim is to capture the rise in stock price when you invest your money. Growth based strategies simply take this a step further and demand that a company has an excellent competitive edge as well as a fair price valuation. This is where growth investing can be contrasted with value investing. Value investors tend to focus quite a bit on the price of the investment.

Let's say there are two companies A and B. Let's say A is a not so great company that is not going to last more than 10 years from the current date. On the other hand, B is a great company that has excellent growth prospects. Currently, A is selling for a price that is worth around 65% of its value, while B is selling for 95% of its value as an investor might calculate it.

The value investor would typically pick A while the growth investor would pick B. This helps highlight one of the biggest advantages of growth investing. It is designed to be a long-term strategy by its very definition. Companies don't grow overnight and in order to realize all of the benefits of the strategies, you need to stay invested for the long-term.

Let's take a look at some of the other advantages of investing this way.

Great Companies

Growth investing strategies place a huge premium on a company remaining competitive over long periods of time. Over the long run, a company's stock price tracks its growth in earnings. Therefore, in order for the price to grow, the earnings have to grow as well at a good pace. The only way this can happen is if the company has a strong competitive edge in the market and in its industry.

All of the big companies you hear about today were once growth-oriented companies. For example, Apple was prototypical growth stock around 2002-2003. The company was gearing up to release its next generation of products and Steve Jobs' vision for the company had only just begun to be fulfilled. The company had a very strong competitive advantage in that it could charge whatever price it wanted for its products and customers were still willing to pay.

In fact, customers were willing to line up for hours outside Apple stores for the products. Any Apple product release was a major event and soon, their products spawned entire side industries such as accessories for iPods and iPhones. The interesting thing was that at no point in this growth journey was Apple stock cheap by standard metrics.

The company sold for a pretty high multiple compared to its earnings. In 2003 the stock closed at $1.05. Today the stock sells for $267.99. Keep in mind that this is after multiple stock splits. Apple issued a 2 for 1 stock split in 2006 and another 7 for 1 stock split in 2014. This means that real gains are well above the difference in stock prices between then and now.

Is Apple still a growth stock? Probably not. It is the biggest company in the world and it has seemingly exhausted its creative ability when it comes to launching earth-shattering products. This is not a bad thing by itself. It is tough for large companies like Apple to keep innovating and disrupting their industries. It is far more profitable for them to simply maintain their position in the industry and consolidate.

My point is that the rewards of growth investing are massive. Just like Apple, Amazon was once a growth stock. Some might argue that it still is a growth stock. Microsoft was once a growth stock, as was Walmart, IBM, Intel, and so on.

Cutting Edge

Growth investing companies tend to maintain their advantage in the market for long periods of time. This is because the industries they operate in tend to be at the forefront of change. Using Apple as an example, once again, the technology industry has seen a massive change from what it used to be at the turn of the millennium.

Growth investing thus helps you capture not just company growth, but you receive the boost of being invested in an entire industry as well. Thus, it isn't as if just one stock is rising, but an entire group of companies are rising. This tends to fuel even more growth since more investors jump into these stocks. Along with Apple, Google, Facebook, Amazon, and Netflix have witnessed huge surges in stock price.

Netflix is a good example of how the rise of an entire sector can help a company. Netflix started off as a small-time competitor of Blockbuster's mail-order movie service. However, they soon pivoted to a streaming service back before anyone even knew what 2G was. Many people did not understand the business model, nor did they grasp the enormity of the CEO, Reed Hastings' vision.

Hastings' bet was to take advantage of the rise of tech services and infrastructure over the last few years of the past decade so as to give Netflix a viable platform. Setting aside the fact that the tech industry lived up to its promise, consider a world where tech companies were not generating any buzz and that Silicon Valley wasn't slowly replacing Wall Street as the economic center of America.

The chances of Netflix succeeding in such an environment would have been extremely low. Without the buzz that was reflected in the company from the rise of tech at large, no one would have paid any deep attention to the rise of the company or its business model. As it stands today, Netflix has many competitors, but it still holds a major place in the hearts and minds of people that buy its services.

This just shows that by following growth investing principles, not only will you find one investment, but you'll end up unearthing an entire world of investments and companies that will rise along with it and take their place in the new economy.

Excitement

This one is counterintuitive but stay with me here. A lot of investors find it difficult to stick to their long-term strategies since they tend to be boring. For example, if you invest in individual stocks that pay good dividends, then you're going to find a lot of your money parked in utility stocks. Utility companies aren't exactly setting the world on fire.

They're in highly regulated industries and their prices are capped. They're safe bets and their earnings are extremely predictable. Their stock prices won't decline too much during bear markets, but neither will they rise too much in bull markets. In short, they're the picture-perfect boring stock. Many investors will find it tough to stick to their discipline and stick to these investments.

They'll crave excitement since this is what the overwhelming messaging with regards to the stock market is. They'll hear their friends and neighbors talking about exciting investments and will want some of that action. As a result, they'll end up switching strategies and will not stick to the long-term holdings rule.

Growth investing mitigates this to a large extent since the companies you will end up unearthing are in exciting and cutting-edge industries. Their stock prices will be volatile. Volatility refers to the degree to which the price moves in either direction. Growth stocks' prices tend to jump around a lot and this provides some sense of entertainment.

The downside is that if they move too far to the downside, investors might sell. However, if the companies choices are right, and if you follow the advice in this part, your downside is going to be limited and this makes it unlikely you'll sell. Instead, you'll see the stock doing something every day and this brings its own sense of validation with it.

Therefore, you're much more likely to stick to your strategy and not end up sabotaging yourself by selling too early.

CHAPTER 23

Stock Picking Strategies

To succeed in stock markets, there are plans you need to master.

Stay flexible: The stock market is a volatile place, which means that, if you ever hope to be successful when investing, then you need to remain ready to pivot at a moment's notice. The market can change in a matter of minutes, which means a stock on a long-running profitability streak can suddenly turn around and become worthless, literally overnight. This means that, if you want to succeed, you are going to need to limit the influence the past has on your decisions and instead focus on the information available in the present and what it will likely mean for the future. Be ready to ditch investments that are turning on you, and reevaluate past choices if you hope to see reliable results in the long term.

Commit to a plan: The plan that you create is going to be critical to your success in the long term, but only if you stick with it every time you choose an investment. While it won't lead you to success with every trade, if you create it using the proper criteria, then it should lead you to make profitable trades more than 50% of the time, which means you will succeed in the end as long as you stick with it religiously.

Furthermore, knowing the acceptable criteria when it comes to selling and buying is crucial to ensure that you will be able to take advantage of emerging trends at a time when it will do you the best.

Have measured expectations: While it is possible to grow rich from investing in the stock market, it is challenging since this kind of growth doesn't happen overnight. Rather, most people who find success there slowly amass assets over time by holding on to profitable trades and getting rid of those that don't pan out before they can generate too much loss.

Additionally, it is likely to take you a prolonged period of time before you get the hang of things, which means you should expect to post a losing record for the first few months you start investing in stocks while you are learning the ropes. Note that this is normal; stick with it if you hope to eventually cross from the red into the black. Going into the process with a realistic idea of what it's going to take to be successful is an ideal way of ensuring that the learning curve will be as manageable as possible.

Choose personalized strategies: Just because you hear about a strategy that is guaranteed to work because someone else found success with it is no real indicator that it is going to work for you. While there is certainly no reason not to give it a try, it is important to ensure that it stands up to your personal standards and matches your natural investment inclinations as well. If it doesn't, the investment will be unlikely to generate the results you need.

Instead, it is always important to be on the lookout for new strategies that line up with your personal inclinations to use as a stepping stone to stock investing success as opposed to barriers that need to be circumvented to see any results. Remaining true to yourself is always going to be the most reliable way to see positive results in the long run.

Be disciplined: It is common for many new traders to go after one type of stock simply because they have a gut feeling about it. The sad truth of the matter is that gut feelings rarely, if ever, payout effectively. As such, if you follow this scattershot approach, you are going to end up making it more difficult to turn a profit in both the short and long-term. What's worse, if you do end up finding success with this process, then all you will be learning is bad habits, which will translate to fewer overall successes in the future. Instead of focusing on your gut, it is important to focus on building the discipline you need to make the right choices, even if your gut is telling you something else. While this will likely be hard at first, it will get easier with time.

Seek absolute truth: It doesn't matter if you feel that the price of a given stock is too low or too high, the only thing you can reliably focus on is its current price. If the facts say that a stock should be valued higher than it currently is, then you will want to buy, and if it is lower, then you will want to sell, end of story. You need to remain impartial about these facts and simply do what they tell you. Developing an attachment to a given stock is only going to hurt your results in the long run.

Focus on logic: After you have formed a successful plan, following it precisely with each trade that you make will always be the most logical next step. This means that, even if the trade doesn't end up working out the way you expected, you should still be pleased with yourself as long as you did what made the most sense at the moment. Going off the book is going to lead to failure far more often than it leads to success. Instead of raging against failed trades, simply look at them as the statistical balance to the other more profitable trades you are likely to make more than 50% of the time, assuming your plan is sound.

Sometimes doing nothing is the right choice: If you have reason to believe a specific stock is overvalued, then you will want to sell; if it is undervalued, then you will want to buy. The same principles go for when a stock is stuck in the middle of the road; the best action is to wait for a stronger signal to appear to indicate a movement in one direction or another. Many new traders find that waiting without making a move is one of the hardest things to do.

Making trades just to trade is always going to be folly. Be patient when the market is stagnant or moving at a faster rate. Wait until things normalize to enjoy reliable profits. Your goal should always be to make trades for the sake of profit, not just to trade for trading's sake.

Understand that there are no sure things: The odds of finding a system that will accurately predict trades

100% of the time, or even 90% of the time, are extremely small. In fact, you have a better chance of winning the lottery or being struck by lightning than of getting anywhere close to those numbers. There are just too many variables to consider at all times, even before you factor in chance and pure, dumb luck. Rather than wasting time looking for the impossible, you will find much better results by looking for a plan that you can rely on and just take the additional loss with a grain of salt.

CHAPTER 24:

Risk Management

There are many different types of risk in the stock market. Some are direct, such as a small company that has the potential to make gains because of innovative products. Others are indirect and external. You can't manage all types of risks. Some come out of the blue, like the 9/11 terrorist attacks or the 2008 financial crash. So, if you think that you can control every form of risk, take a deep breath and realize you can't. We are going to try and describe every major category of risk investor face, and if possible, we'll suggest ways to deal with them.

Emotional and Person Risk

First and foremost, you can control the risks to your investments that come from personal factors. These include fear, impatience, and greed. Emotions like these can be hard to control, but learning to take charge of them is essential if you are going to be a successful investor. When real money is on the line, these emotions can become strong and overpowering. You must not let that happen.

The most common problem when it comes to emotions and personal risk is fear. When a stock market starts looking bearish, many investors immediately jump ship. They are making a huge mistake. A good investor is not getting in and out of the market at the slightest sign of a problem. In fact, selling off when everyone else is could be one of the biggest mistakes individual investors make. By the way, that doesn't exempt large investors. Many professional traders are subject to the same emotions and exhibit the same behavior during downturns. Massive sell-offs causes bear markets to develop.

First of all, remember that you are looking to hold your investments over the long term. So, ups and downs of the market and even recessions are not a reason to sell them. Over the past 50 years, by far, the worst stock market contraction happened in the 2008 financial crisis. However, even that was short-lived. People that sold off their investments were either faced with being out of the markets altogether or having to get back in the markets when prices were appreciating. The lifetimes of other major bear markets were similar or even more short-lived. The first lesson in managing personal risk is to hold your investments through downturns.

The second lesson is that rather than giving into fear, you should start to see market downturns as opportunities. When prices are rapidly dropping due to a market sell-off, you should be buying shares. It's impossible to know where the bottom of a market is, and you shouldn't concern yourself with that. At any time that share prices are declining, it's an opportunity, and so you should be making regular stock purchases. In one year, two years, or five years down the road, on average, the stocks that you purchased in a downturn are going to be worth quite a bit more.

The second problem that arises as a part of personal risk is greed. Many people start seeing dollar signs when they begin investing. Having a get rich quick mentality is not compatible with successful investing. Your approach should be centered on slowly and steadily accumulating wealth and not making a quick buck. As you invest, you're going to be coming across claims that certain trades or stocks are the next best thing, but you're better off ignoring such claims. More often than not, they turn out to be false. The stock market is not a gambling casino, even though many people treat it that way. You can avoid succumbing to greed by maintaining a regular investment program and not being taken in by the temptation that you can profit from short-term swings or "penny stocks" that are going to supposedly take off.

Finally, there is the related problem of impatience. After the Great Depression, people developed a more reasonable and cautious approach to the stock market. They realized that you're not going to get rich in six months or a year. The idea of long-term investing became dominant.

Unfortunately, in recent years, this lesson seems to be getting lost. More people are behaving like traders rather than as investors. Far too many investors are being taken in by the seduction of being able to beat market returns. Instead of being impatient, you should realize that you're in it for the long haul. Rather than trying to make a few extra bucks now, you're seeking to build wealth.

Risk of Loss of Capital

Obviously, financial risk is something you face when investing. Theoretically, there is a chance that you will lose all the money you invest in the stock market. This can happen if you tie your fate to a small number of companies. Several well-known companies like Lumber Liquidators, Bear-Stearns, and GM have either had major problems or gone completely under. Investors may have lost large sums in the process. The way to deal with this is to avoid investing in a small number of companies.

You'll also want to pay attention to the types of companies you invest in. Putting all of your money into small-cap stocks, for example, is probably a bad idea. So is putting all of your money into emerging markets, or into one sector of the stock market. Again, the key message is diversification. It's the way to protect you from financial risk.

Market and Economic Risk

Some factors are beyond your control, and the economy inevitably cycles through slowdowns and downturns. The market will cycle along with the economy, and also experiences crash when the economy may be doing fine overall.

171

Political Risk and Government

Government and politics can create big risks in the stock market. International events can cause market crashes, and these days even a tweet from the President can cause markets to rise and fall. Lately, some politicians have also been talking about breaking up the big tech companies. Others are talking about investigating them. Such talk–and worse actions–can have a negative impact on the markets. Part of your job as an investor is to keep a close eye on the news. You're going to want to know what's happening so that you can adjust if necessary.

Inflation Risk

Inflation hasn't been high in decades. However, in the late 1970s, inflation rates were routinely in the double digits. Hopefully, that isn't going to be something that happens anytime soon, because high inflation rates can eat your returns alive. If the stock market is appreciating at 7% per year, but inflation is 14%, you can see that it's like having debt, but investing in stocks–it's a losing proposition. Right now, inflation risk is very low, but you'll want to have some awareness of it and always keep tabs on it. High inflation rates also tend to go hand-in-hand with high-interest rates, since the Federal Reserve will raise rates to try and slow down inflation. That means that bonds might become more attractive when inflation gets out of control.

Risk vs. Return

One of the fundamental trade-offs that an investor will make is a risk vs. return. Generally speaking, the higher the risk, the greater the possibility of good returns. In 1998, Amazon was a pretty high-risk investment. While it had potential, major bookstores like Borders and Barnes & Noble dominated the space. Amazon was on shaky ground at the time, and another company could have come in and competed successfully for online book sales. That never happened, and Amazon ended up dominating book sales and expanding widely across retail and into cloud computing. That risk has translated into massive returns. A $10,000 investment in 1998 would be worth more than $1 million today.

But hindsight is 20/20. Today, there are similar opportunities all around us, but it's hard to know which ones are going to end up being successful over the long term. If you are an aggressive investor, part of your job is going to be estimating which companies are the best bets for the future.

Risk vs. return also plays a role in emerging markets. These countries may experience massive GDP growth year after year since they have lots of room to grow. Domestic companies that are growing with their economies can offer remarkable returns. However, there are many risks. Rapid growth can often evaporate with major downturns. Stability is lower in emerging markets; you could face complete loss of capital.

These examples serve to illustrate why a diversified portfolio is essential.

Managing Risk

There are a few time-tested strategies that have been developed that help manage risk. They even minimize, as much as possible, the kinds of risk that you will face that are completely out of control. That could include anything from a terrorist attack to interest rate changes.

These strategies are simple and easy to understand. The problem is that in practice, many investors fail to follow them, and instead let their decision making be guided by emotions. You might end up following that path as well. However, we are going to give you the tools you need to avoid it. It's up to you whether you utilize them or not.

Dollar-Cost Averaging

The strategy seeks to avoid being impacted by the ups and downs of the market. You don't know when you are buying at the top of a market or the bottom. None of us has a crystal ball, but what we can do is average out our investments over the long-term. You can do this using a technique called dollar-cost averaging, which is simply buying shares at regular intervals–completely ignoring price fluctuations. Most ups and downs in the stock market are actually noise. So, you should avoid worrying about them as much as possible. And we've already noted that stock goes up and down with bull and bear markets. Using dollar-cost averaging, you remove the stress (and hence the emotion) that is associated with these fluctuations. The costs are averaged out because sometimes you are going to be buying when prices are low, even though at other times, you will be buying when prices are relatively high.

Speaking of rising share prices, this technique also helps you avoid another emotional problem. If share prices are rising, many investors panic. The reason they panic is they are worried that share prices will rise to new heights and never come back down again. They will "miss an opportunity" of gains, and also be forced into a position of having to buy shares at higher prices.

Those short-term ups and downs don't matter over the long-term. Whether Amazon had a long gain 4 years ago or not won't matter to the investor using dollar-cost averaging. All that matters is the long-term trend—and regularly purchasing shares along the way. Looking at the chart below, we've used an arrow to show Amazon's long-term trend and circled a few of the short-term fluctuations that, at the time, caused a great deal of angst and anxiety. Traders probably tried to profit from them. But look how small they are, compared to the overall picture.

CHAPTER 25

Diversification

The first strategy that is used when investing in the long-term is diversification. Put simply, this means investing in more than one company. Preferably, you would invest in multiple companies and do so among different industries and sectors. The purpose of using this type of strategy is to avoid going down with a sinking ship.

However, a company doesn't have to go under to hurt your portfolio. Instead, it may stagnate, and a stagnant investment might not be able to provide you with the dollars that you need in order to have a successful and secure retirement. You need investments that are going to grow over time.

The fact is that it's inevitable that certain investments are going to fail. Over the long term, it's not likely that there is going to be a catastrophic collapse of a company, although that does sometimes happen. In most cases, a company will fail to keep up. It is stock price will languish or decline, even in absolute terms and not just in terms of where it should be in order to keep up with inflation. This is the most likely scenario you will encounter.

Some companies decline in relative importance but remain good investments. Examples include Intel, Microsoft and IBM. All three companies remain solid investments, even though they are not the machines they once were that completely dominated the economy. IBM has reinvented itself and pursued many different directions since exiting the PC business, focusing on selling business services and machine intelligence, among other things. It remains a cutting-edge research firm when it comes to specialties like AI, and while it is stock isn't poised for aggressive growth, it does show growth and they pay a good dividend payment. Microsoft continues to benefit from the dominance of the Windows operating system on desktop and laptop computers, but they have also diversified into areas like cloud computing. Microsoft, however, got left behind by the mobile wars and isn't nearly as important as it once was. When you hear big tech mentioned these days, you rarely hear Microsoft mentioned, the focus is on Facebook, Amazon, Google, Netflix, and Microsoft's former rival, Apple.

Does that mean these companies are not good to invest in? Absolutely not. They would have been and still are solid investments to keep in your portfolio, but they are examples of companies that once seemed completely dominant and invincible that have become mature and steady companies that are good investments, but not the tops in the economy anymore.

But as we've seen, some companies–even formerly reliable ones–go completely belly up. GM needed a bailout to avoid bankruptcy, and had you sunk all of your stock in GM in the years prior to it is near demise, you would have possibly suffered major losses. While companies that become that large are not likely to completely fail, it does happen sometimes and you can't know which companies that are going to happen to five, ten, or twenty years down the road. For that reason, it's important to spread your investments over a wide range of companies.

Industry sectors can also pose a risk as well. Sometimes, a given industry or sector may experience it is own "bear market" while other sectors and industries are doing well. In addition, over time, many industries may fade away or become irrelevant. The coal industry may be heading in that direction now, but the horse and buggy whip industries in the face of the development of the automobile is a classic example. Something that drastic isn't likely to happen very often, but the risk is always going to be there, and so you don't want to sink all of your investments into one single business sector.

Company size is also a factor that needs to be considered. Companies can be divided according to large-cap, mid-cap, and small-cap. In addition, there is also now a "mega-cap" category. To determine where a company fits, a determination of their market capitalization is made. This is the price per share of the company's stock multiplied by the number of shares "outstanding" (that is shares on the market). These are broken down as follows:

Large-cap: This is a company with $10 billion or more in market capitalization.

Mid-cap: These companies have a market worth of $2 billion up to $10 billion.

Small-cap: A small-cap company is one with a market capitalization less than $2 billion.

Mega-cap: This category is reserved for behemoths like Apple and Google (Alphabet), that are companies worth $200 billion or more.

Micro-cap: This is another sometimes used subcategory, these are small-cap stocks that have a market capitalization that is below $300 million. There are also "nano-cap" stocks that are worth less than $50 million.

Large-cap stocks tend to be stable and mature companies, and many of them pay dividends. Or else they are very large and rapidly growing, like Amazon and Netflix.

S&P SmallCap 600 vs. S&P 500 - 20 Years

The massive growth of small cap funds compared to the S & P 500.

When deciding on what mix to invest in, the general rule, although it's certainly not exclusive, is to consider mid-caps and small-caps stocks to be higher risk. It's far more likely that a small-cap company will fail, in fact it might not even make the news. So, your real investment risk might be investing in small, micro, and Nano-cap companies.

However, where there is risk there is also large potential for growth. A mid-cap or small-cap company has a lot of room to grow. Many of them are tomorrow's large-cap companies. Of course, it may be difficult to determine which ones are going to play this role, but that is part of the investment game.

That another way to diversify is to split up your portfolio among companies that have different amounts of market capitalization. You can put some of your investments into large-cap companies, some into mid-cap companies, and so on. The amounts allocated to different companies will depend on your overall investment goals. Generally speaking, those seeking less investment risk and less aggressive growth are going to invest more, or even all of their investments in large-cap companies. On the other hand, those who are seeking more aggressive growth who also have a higher tolerance of risk are going to be willing to put more investments into small-cap and mid-cap companies.

Of course, none of this represents rules that are cast in stone. Some of the companies that we've mentioned like Amazon, Apple, or Netflix are high-growth companies that are also large-cap stocks. Tesla is another example, it's a large-cap stock that also has massive potential for growth since few people have moved into purchasing electric cars yet. It also represents huge risk; the goals of the company may never be materialized.

A plan of diversification should include about 15-20 companies, that are spread across different sectors and industries as well as having a mix of large-cap, mid-cap, and small-cap company sizes if you want some growth power in your portfolio. You don't want to have too many companies in your portfolio, or you might get yourself in a situation where it's not possible to do proper analysis and track them to make sure that you have good investments.

Many investors prefer to get diversification using exchange-traded funds. But for now, be aware that you can use exchange-traded funds to get a great deal more diversity than you could possibly get from investing in 10-20 companies on your own. One way to handle this situation is to mix it up, maybe you invest in your top ten favorite companies and then put the rest of your investment dollars into exchange-traded funds that will diversify your portfolio.

The bottom line is you want to create an investment portfolio that can weather one, two, or possibly three companies you've invested in not going well. Of course, keep in mind that you can get out of investments that are not doing well. If an investment is not helping you meet your goals, you should sell the shares when it's feasible and put your investment dollars elsewhere.

There are many scenarios that we could imagine so that you can see the value of diversification. If you put all of your money into coal companies, in ten years, you might be in a situation where they are all bankrupt. Or, you could invest in just about five small-cap companies, and then you find one does well over the long term, 2 loose value, and 2 actually go under. That is not a recipe for building wealth over the long term.

But instead, if you had invested in ten large-cap companies and five index funds in addition to your small-cap companies, then the damage that the failing small-caps would have caused to your portfolio would be limited and contained, and chances are the gains that you would have from your other investments would have massively outpaced the losses.

Diversification Also Means Going Outside Stocks

Most investors are not going to want to be entirely in stocks. You are also going to want to have at least some of your money invested in bonds, precious metals, real estate, and other assets. So, when you set up your diversification strategy, you are going to want to decide what if any other types of asset classes you want to include in your portfolio, and then divide them up by percentages. There are many online resources from financial experts and large companies like Vanguard and Fidelity that you can use as guidelines in order to determine how to allocate your portfolio to meet different investment goals.

CHAPTER 26:

Mindset and Psychology

Traders must have a certain mindset when it comes to investing. Investing in stock takes a lot of self-discipline. There is a certain psychology that traders must become familiar with to be successful in their investments. There is a whole investing mindset that must be utilized to drive results. Investors must detach themselves from their emotions when investing in stock; otherwise, they risk trading out of fear and greed. Investors must also not become too attached to any stock. Although there is an art to investing, it is important that investors utilize logic to drive their actions.

Self-Discipline

Self-discipline is crucial when it comes to investing. Investors must be able to follow their plans and achieve their goals. However, many investors become tempted by the idea of better performance and abandon all logic in hopes of achieving greater returns on their investments. They will use emotions when it comes to market conditions. They may also incur greater costs because of a lack of discipline. Investors must stick with their original plan despite temptations otherwise. A short-term sacrifice will be worth it in the long-term. Although it may not be the most appealing path, the disciplined path is most often the most successful path, especially when it comes to trading.

Following the original plan and goals that the investor set is crucial. Although there are situations in which it may be more beneficial to adjust the plans due to a highly changing market or personal financial misfortune, it is better to stick to the original plan most of the time. Once the investor strays from the path originally, it will become easier to repeat that action and abandon all original plans. The investor may act without using logic and end up incurring great losses. When this happens, however, investors fail to see the consequences of their actions in the long-term. Stocks that the investors should have held onto could have resulted in gains, but the investor chose to incur losses because of a lack of discipline instead. The investor opens themselves up to allowing for loopholes whenever they deem necessary, and they hurt themselves in the long-term. The investor should create a plan for what to do if the market is negative and stick to this. They should create this plan beforehand so that they are not biased at all. However, the real discipline is actually following through with this plan when the time comes.

The investor should also be disciplined in their amount of investments. Instead of deciding last-minute use the money that they planned to set aside for stock on spending, they should stick to the original plan. It is quite easy to say that one will not invest this week and get right back to it the next week, but they have already fallen off of the plan. This can discourage the investor and lead to further lack of discipline in the future. The best way to avoid this from happening is to stick with the plan in the first place.

The investor must not change their portfolio based on recent market activities. This can prove to be quite difficult, especially in a bear market. However, it is usually worth it to stick through the hard times and wait for another period of growth. One's portfolio should be managed and properly rebalanced as necessary. Although it may be tempting to change this based on market conditions, the investor must hold out through the rough times. If investing for the long-term, the investor must ensure that the investments are, indeed, kept for the long-term.

Trading Psychology

The psychology that goes into trading encompasses several factors. The trader must be able to control their emotions, make quick decisions, and remain disciplined. Of course, this is in addition to being able to understand companies and predict the direction in which the stock will go. With enough practice and research, anyone can master the technical side of trading. It's those who master the psychological side that is truly successful in trading. This is what separates the good traders from the great traders. Trading psychology can be a skill crafted by practice, but it also requires the trader to shift their way of thinking.

Traders must understand the emotions that go into trading. By first understanding them, they will allow themselves to become more skillful in the way they handle such emotions. Traders must realize that fear is a natural response to bad news about the stock market. It is natural that traders will feel a sense of urgency and be tempted to liquidate their holdings, reduce risk, or otherwise sell their stocks. This, at the time, seems to be a wise move. However, traders must make decisions quickly that will benefit them in the long term, not satisfy their emotions in the short-term. By doing so, they may risk losses, but they will not miss out on the gains that they otherwise would miss out on had they given in to their emotions. It is important for traders to realize that fear stems from what people believe is a threat to them. In this instance, the threat is to their money.

In addition to overcoming fear, investors must know how to overcome greed. If an investor holds onto a winning stock for too long, trying to get every possible amount of money they can, these gains may quickly turn to losses. Holding onto a stock for too long can prove to be less profitable than one may imagine. Yet again, traders must come up with a plan ahead of time. They must know when the right time to let go of a stock is. At the time, it seems like a wise move to the investor. They may earn more, do better than they originally thought, and make more gains. This sometimes occurs. Most of the time, however, greed is not the right choice. Traders must distinguish between greed and making wise decisions based on market changes. Sometimes, it is better to stray from the original plan. What often occurs, however, is that emotion interferes with logic, and the investor makes an unwise move by listening to their heart instead of their head.

Investors must create an extensive plan and set rules for themselves. Instead of "going with the flow," it's important to have a step-by-step plan for the investor's trading endeavors. This should be based on rational decisions, not spur-of-the-moment emotions or instincts. They must plan out when they will enter a trade and when they will exit a trade. This must be followed no matter what, and this is a great way to eliminate emotional bias. The trader may plan for certain occurrences. If unpredictable earnings occur, whether positive or negative, the trader may establish exceptions to their plan should these occur. The trader may buy a security if certain macroeconomic events occur. They may also set limits to eliminate fear and greed. These should be upper and lower limits. The upper limits will eliminate greed, and the lower will limit fear. If such a limit is reached, the trader may stop their activities for the day to eliminate emotions from taking over their activities.

On the other hand, traders should not rationalize their mistakes. Although it is important to not dwell on the past and all of the possible ways that the trader messed up in, the trader should still recognize that they made mistakes. This is important for self-improvement, as there will always be ways in which the trader could have conducted their trades more efficiently or effectively. As a result, the trader should definitely analyze what did go wrong every time period that they wish to do so. This will make the trader better and improve their future performance and decision-making skills.

Investing Mindset

Traders may also learn different mindsets from other traders. By researching extensively and hearing how other people conduct their trades, there is much to learn. By increasing knowledge, the investor may decrease their negative emotional reactions. They will further understand the stock market and how it operates, and this will help to eliminate such reactions.

Although it is important to stick to one's plan, traders must adopt flexible mindsets. They must be willing to try new tools, buy and sell new stocks, research new companies, and trade differently. There is no "correct" way to trade. There are simply many different ways of doing so. Some may be more profitable than others. Some may work well for one trader and not well for another. Traders should be willing to slightly experiment to see what the best way for them to trade is. This may also decrease emotion when it comes to stock.

Investors should also be critical of themselves and view their trading from a logical stance. There will be certain ways to trade that will result in greater returns. Traders must be willing to reflect on their performance and see what resulted in gains and what didn't. There is always room for improvement, and traders must recognize that. Perhaps for one time period, the trader wasn't researching as thoroughly and missed certain aspects that they should have spent more time on. Perhaps the trader did let emotion influence their trades. By recognizing potential bad habits, the trader will be able to work on improving themselves and making themselves a more profitable and skillful trader for the future.

Traders must use technical analysis to drive their investing decisions. There are various ways of doing so. Perhaps the trader wishes to focus on charts. This can prove highly beneficial for seeing a visual representation of performance. The trader may have a group of investors that they seek advice from with their trades. They may have a journal to write their plan in. There are programs to use to help with investments. Whichever way the trader prefers that they conduct their business, there should be some sort of support to help logically analyze their decisions. There must be a guide.

Detaching Emotion from Stock

Emotions and trading simply don't mix. In addition to greed and fear, traders must be willing not to get attached to their stocks. Stock investments will constantly change. There will be times where it is the wisest move to invest in one stock and not another. However, traders will often become quite attached to a particular stock. The investor must be able to let go of stocks that simply aren't beneficial for them to hold on to. There is no guarantee for how well a stock will perform, as the market is constantly changing, and stocks will change, too. Investors must separate themselves from their stocks and learn when to let a particular stock go.

When trading, it is important to separate logic from emotion. Trading is a numbers game. It's all about what will benefit the trader in the long-term. While it may be easy to let fear or greed take over, to let one's mistakes hinder their future performance, or to become attached to a particular stock, these are not beneficial for one's performance. The trader must adopt a certain mindset and familiarize themselves with the proper psychology of trading. Doing so will prove highly beneficial to the trader.

CHAPTER 27:

Trading Strategies

N ow that you know how to choose your stocks, it's time to learn the strategies that can help you optimize your chances of earning good money from stocks. Take note that the returns on stocks aren't guaranteed and as mentioned earlier, are subject to market risks or the risk of incurring losses because of unfavorable movements or changes in stock prices. The best you can do is to use strategies that can minimize the risk and amount of possible losses and maximize your chances and the number of profits you can make.

Define Your Profit Goal and Stop-loss Limits

When it comes to stock market trading, one of the worst enemies you can have are your emotions. Believe me when I say that my emotions had gotten the better of me in the past when it came to trade in stocks, and in most cases, those moments resulted in losses. As such, it's important to have an objective basis for your trading decisions. And one of them is defining your profit goals.

If you plan to trade on a very regular basis, say daily or weekly, a relatively lower profit goal is ideal. A 5% to 10% profit target for a day or week is neither too lofty nor too low and can be achieved with timely trades. This means that when your stocks' prices reach a level where your expected profit (net of commissions from buying and selling them) reaches your profit goal, you should sell the stock already. Don't give greed the chance to lose that profit and regardless of how you feel, make it a commitment to follow your profit goals and sell once they're achieved. If you are taking the longer-term, buy-and-hold approach, you can aim for a much higher profit goal because of the relatively long-time frame.

Aside from defining your profit goals at which to sell your stocks, you should also establish a stop-loss limit, which is a price at which your maximum expected net loss–taking into consideration the commissions paid for both buying and selling the stock. How much should your stop-loss limits be? It would depend on the amount of cash you're comfortable losing. If you're comfortable with losing 5%, then let it be a rule that when your stock's price drops to a level where you're expected net loss–taking into consideration the commissions for buying and selling–will be 5%, you'll sell the stock. Do it regardless of how you feel. It will help you move on faster.

Why a stop-loss limit? It's because having no such limits can worsen your losses. It's like diving off a bottomless pit. By limiting your losses, you can live to trade another day–or hour.

Cost Averaging

This refers to a strategy wherein you bring down the average purchase cost of your stock during downward trending markets, i.e., bear markets, so that you can make it easier to make profits later on when the market reverses back to an upward trend, i.e., bull market. Here's how it works.

Let's say you bought ten shares of stocks of Apple, Inc. at $100 per share for a total buying cost of $1,000. Please take note that since this is just for illustration purposes, I have intentionally left out commissions charged by the broker and other incidental expenses. Let's say after a week, its price goes down to $90. That will give you a loss of $10 per share or a total expected loss–again, not factoring in commissions and other expenses for the sake of simplicity–of $100 or 10%. You have two ways to go about this.

First is to wait for stock prices to go back up by $10 to $100 per share so that you can break even. And if you want to make a profit of say 5%, you'll need prices to go up to $105 per share.

The other way to go about this is to use the cost-averaging strategy, in which you buy more shares of Apple, Inc. stocks at the $90 price. Let's say you bought ten more shares at $90 per share that'll cost you $900. You'll then have a total of 20 shares with a total cost of $1,900 and if you average that, your average buying cost per share would go down to only $95 from $100 originally. This is good news! Why?

Because your average buying cost drops to just $95 per share, you'll no longer have to wait for prices to go back up to $100 per share to break even. You need to wait for it to climb up to $95! Even better, when prices come back up to $100, you'll already make a profit of $100 or a 5.26% profit.

You can also use the cost averaging strategy if you choose to go long term, i.e., use the buy-and-hold stock market investing approach. Many people choose a very good stock, buy them, and buy some more as time goes by when funds become available. When the market goes up, they automatically make profits. When the market goes down, all the more they have the opportunity to make their future profits bigger and average buying costs lower.

Short Selling

You can still make money even when the prices of stocks are going down, i.e., during a bear market. How? By selling stocks, you don't have and buy them back later on at much lower prices. That is called short selling. The reason it's called short selling is that you're selling stocks that you don't have at the moment–you're short of stocks! This is how it works.

Let's say the price of Apple's stocks is on a downward trend. Say it's currently doing at $95.00 per share and based on technical analysis and market chatter, there's a very strong chance that its price will fall back down further to around $85.00 per share. You can sell 10 shares of Apple stocks you don't own yet, then buy them back later in the day or the week–depending on your arrangements with your chosen stock brokerage company—at a much lower price like $85.00 per share, which will give you a profit of about $10.00 per share or a total profit of $100. And you can do this even when prices are falling! You can only profit from short-selling when prices are going down.

You may be thinking: won't I go to jail selling something I don't have? Well, you won't because technically, you won't be shortchanging your counterparties. It's because brokerage houses that allow short-selling has a securities lending facility, where you can "borrow" shares of stocks that you don't have yet to sell on the market. When the price of the stock you short-sold drops further, you can buy from the market so you can pay back your broker for the shares of stock you borrowed. It's that simple. That's why short selling won't get you jailed!

Buy-And-Hold

This last trading strategy is the long-haul approach and is often referred to as a passive type of stock market investing. In case you've already forgotten, the reason why the buy-and-hold strategies considered a passive investment strategy is that it involves much less work compared to an active trading strategy where you'll have to monitor the market frequently and execute trades. And as the name implies, all you'll need to do with this type of investing strategy is to do your initial research, buy your stocks, and go about your life with very minimal monitoring.

With a buy-and-hold approach, you'll need to monitor your stocks every month if only to be updated. It won't even hurt you much if you monitor it once or twice a year because you're in it for the long walk and market fluctuations wouldn't matter much. The most crucial task–and probably the only cumbersome one–that you'll have to perform when with a buy-and-hold approach is the initial research. Because you won't be actively monitoring and managing stocks under this approach, you'll have to choose stocks that are fundamentally sound and have solid financial bases for substantial capital appreciation. To this end, blue-chip stocks are often the best ones to go for.

CHAPTER 28:

Monitoring Your Investments

After making your stock market investments, it is important to monitor and keep track of these investments so that you can be aware of how they are performing and whether they are on track to meet your financial goals. Monitoring also allows you to make more informed decisions on whether to sell or hold on to your investments. We are going to take a look at how to monitor your investments.

Stock Monitoring Activities

Below are some steps you should take to monitor the stocks you are invested in.

Check Stock Tables

Stock tables are a great way to find out useful information about your stock, its trading activity, changes in value, and other stats. You should get into the habit of checking them out. If you are investing for the long-term, this can be done at least once a week. If you are a more active trader, you should check out stock tables every day.

Compare Your Stock to Benchmarks

Benchmarks are indices representing a specific sector or the entire market. Benchmarks are used to show the general performance of a particular sector or the whole market. Checking how your stock is performing in comparison to appropriate benchmarks will tell you whether things are moving in the right direction or not. For instance, if you notice that your stock is consistently performing lower than the benchmark for its sector, this is an indication that you need to start thinking about selling that stock.

Study Your Account Statements

You should regularly re-read the account statements you receive from your broker. As you do this, look at the performance of your investments, as well as the costs you are paying out to your broker. Remember, the costs paid out to your broker have a significant impact on your profits. You should also check whether the performance of your stocks is in line with your financial goals.

Stay Up-To-Date with Company News

Keep yourself updated on any news affecting the companies you have invested in. Read their news and press releases, check out the noticeboard on their websites, and check for company-related news from third-party sources such as trading sites, industry magazines, news websites, and so on. When checking out the news, watch out for things like changes in senior management, mergers and acquisitions, and any other corporate changes. Such information will give you an idea of the direction the company is headed, which in turn will make it easier for you to make decisions on whether to hold or sell the company's stock.

To make the task of keeping up with company news easier for yourself, you can set up Google alerts for the companies you have invested in. This way, you will receive any news about these companies directly to your email.

Follow General Economic News

In addition to news related to the companies you have invested in, you should also keep yourself up-to-date with market news and general news that may have an impact on the economy. Is the stock market on a bull or a bear run? Is there inflation in the country? What is the political environment like in the country? Is there a looming war? How is the dollar performing against other currencies? All these factors have an impact on the economy and the stock market, which means that they also have an impact on your portfolio.

Check Your Indicators

You should periodically study the indicators that you used to evaluate the value of your stocks before you purchased the stocks and check whether there are any significant changes in these indicators. If there are positive changes, you can continue holding onto the stock. If the changes are negative, on the other hand, this is a signal that you need to sell.

Go Through the Quarterly Reports

We saw earlier that publicly listed companies are required to release their earnings reports every quarter. Once the reports are released, take time to go through the reports of the companies in your portfolio. If the reports show good performance, you can hold on to the stock. If the reports show poor performance, then this should be a cause for worry. However, don't sell your stocks just because of poor performance in a single quarter. Even the best-performing companies experience a slump in business sometimes. However, if poor performance is posted consistently, it might be time to reconsider the stock.

Weekly Stock Performance Reporting

Most stockbrokers, especially online brokers, will also provide you with performance reports which give you an overview of your investments over time. You should go through these reports at least weekly. However, most brokers will allow you to customize the period you want the report to cover, with the time periods ranging anywhere from a week to a couple of years. From the report, you can glean the value of your investments at the beginning of the time period, as well as the current value.

In addition to showing you the performance of your investments over time, these reports also allow you to compare how your investments have performed against a benchmark symbol over time. This allows you to know how your stocks are faring against the general market.

CHAPTER 29:

Money Management

The value of money management for being a good trader cannot be emphasized sufficiently. Speaking of a person's day trading process, a person has to have a very stringent method of money management. It should initially be decided how much you will risk and keep to this amount in your day-to-day trading efforts.

Day trading is already competitive and every day, computer-operated algorithmic trades are making it even more complex. Many traders invest bigger in their day trading account or involve in short-term trading or even gambling and tend to lose more money. Awareness about market terms like tender price, ask for price and exit and entry price is extremely important for making the most of money management. You will exchange more profitably as you gain more experience and expertise.

The long-lived advice of "plan your trade and trade your plan" is another important and essential step in becoming a successful trader. Since these reduce the chances of losing money, the odds of your profits are maximized in every exchange.

To gain optimum profits through trading, always plan first since it is already known that; if you fail to plan, you plan to fail. You will end up making a loss if you lose confidence in your skills and your trading strategy, and particularly if you hold a position in the market. You have to manage trading so as to make a profit at the end of the day despite all the losses faced. You need to grasp how trading strategies operate during the day.

A successful trader has to put in money and time despite all the best instruments and trade strategies. Many traders mistakenly think they can generate money without investing in a huge effort by following some wonderful strategy. They need to understand that behaving with rapacity; panic and selfishness contribute to a stock market collapse. It is better to learn which trading strategy and techniques of market money management work best with your type of trading.

Important Money Management Rules for Traders

As a trader, you also manage your financial burden and decide with respect to your risk tolerance scale. To protect your investments, to maximize profits and to reduce your losses, the following rules for managing your money may be pursued:

Practice Trade Sizing

Do not invest more than 10% of your stock trading capital in a single trade, for example, if you have a capital of $25,000, you may not use more than $2500 in any one of your trades.

Keep Strict Stop-losses

It is recommended to set the minimum mental stop-loss of 10% and a hard stop-loss of at least 20% on inventories worth more than $10. A mental stop-loss means that the loss you make with respect to a particular stock cannot exceed 10%. Assume that you evaluate your portfolio at the end of the day and note that one stock is showing a loss greater than 10%. You must then look at the product closely, and study the reports about the related company to see what caused this drop in the price of your products. On the other side, hard stop-losses are legitimate stop orders placed by the traders. These often serve as a means of protection if there is an unpredicted shift in the market behavior.

Book Profits

Partial profits are best attained at 40% or higher. It implies that you should sell part of the stock if it shows a rise of 40% or more and hold the part of the stock for later trading. You can recover the amount equal to or more than your initial investment in this way.

Trailing Profits

After making a profit of 15%, push your stop-loss to the point of break-even and as long as you are in that position, try to achieve that; hence this is called trailing stop. You will consider using such a strategy following the initial benefit of 15%.

Stay Away from Margin Trading

It is significant to use margin trading sensitively to prevent suffering from the loss greater than your initial investment. Speaking of margins, they are usually a good way to grow your wealth in primary stocks. But on the other hand, such a stock investment technique may lead quickly to huge losses if not carefully observed and properly performed. The sayings of a recognized trader can be quoted to sum this up. He said that bigger issues arise when one assumes bigger positions.

Small and Steady Wins Race

Begin with little money and slowly but steadily grow your self-confidence and your business account. Don't aspire immediately to get wealthy. You could gradually increase your capital exposure if you have continuous trade returns following a long period (more than one year), particularly if you remained consistent even when the market is facing hard times.

Diversify

Let us assume that you have invested in 20 stocks following the rule of diversity and invested only 5% of your capital in each stock, and one of your options unexpectedly fails and you suffer a total loss with respect to that particular stock. This implies that just 5% of your market profits would have been wasted. You can survive and trade without serious harm. By contrast, if you do not have an effective money management strategy and there is less diversity in your transactions, bringing your entire capital to single trades will keep your profits going, and ultimately most of your trading capital can be lost. You might even be removed from the exchanges altogether.

Control your Risk

It is advised to continue with a paper exchange practice program if you're new in trading. Keep your stock trading records in writing and track record all the feelings and errors you are experiencing during your business. After about a month, you are ready to trade with cash in reality. Do remember that major positions cause large problems.

Use Limit Orders to Get in and Get out of Position

You may be provided with opportunities for trading in the market, however, the price may be different from your desired one. Most of the time, a limit order put close to the last closure is typically met since a stock normally retraces after the first part of the session.

Some traders cannot manage checking the stock throughout the day. The solution to this problem is the market order. Note that there may be fluctuation in the price you had to pay when your order is done.

The biggest mistake investors make is to blindly follow a trade process. Despite the definite course of a process, several variables involved in the process must be considered.

Keep an Eye on Brokerage

Brokerage is the biggest eater of your investments, although it is not taken seriously. Brokerage may involve concealed charges that may consume your profits and enhance your losses. The brokers sometimes behave selfishly and conceal the schemes that are profitable for you and offer the schemes bringing profits to them. This implies that it is important to check the brokerage schemes personally and not to blindly accept the schemes offered by the broker. Moreover, the trading statement must also be checked.

CHAPTER 30:

Common Mistakes and How to Avoid Them

As a beginner, the rules of day trading may seem a bit foreign and hard to work with. You want to make sure you are getting into the market and doing well, but you also worry this is going to be too hard to maintain and that the market will move fast. The market does move fast, but there are a lot of great strategies, including some of the great ones we talk about in this guidebook, that can help you get started.

Because of the fast movement of the market and the fact that it is hard to predict what will happen in the stock market, there are a lot of mistakes that a beginner can make when it comes to working in this kind of market. These mistakes can cost the beginner a lot of money and can make it so they can no longer play in the market at all.

Just because you are a beginner doesn't mean that you automatically have to fall prey to some of these mistakes. You just need to recognize what they are and learn how to avoid them as much as possible. Keep in mind through all of this that even traders who have been in the market for a long time make mistakes or have the market turn against them, and they lose money.

We can look at some of these common mistakes and at least put them down to a minimum, allowing us to keep more money in the process. Some of the common mistakes beginners often make, and how we can avoid them to see more success with day trading include:

Not Setting Your Stop-losses

The first mistake we need to take a look at here is the stop-loss rules. These are all about protecting you and making sure that you keep things safe with a market that is moving all the time. The stop-loss on one side will make sure that if the trend goes in the wrong direction, the market will pull you out, so you don't lose too much money. The stop-loss on the other side will make sure that you can pull out with some profits before that upward trend reverses itself.

When a stock starts to drop, some of the newer traders will start to panic because they see they are losing money. They decide to hold the stock, instead of exiting when they reach this stop-loss point. You should pick that stop-loss point, and stick with it no matter what to help protect your investment. Sometimes the trend will reverse, and the money will come back to you. Often it will continue, and you will lose more money in the process. And it doesn't take long for a bad trade to leave you broke.

Set that stop-loss point before you ever enter the trade, and then stick with it. This helps you to take some of the emotions out of the trade and will help you to get out. Sure, you will lose money, but you will lose a lot less with this method than if you hold onto the stock and don't get out on time.

These stop-losses are so nice for making sure that your emotions will not get into the trading. As soon as those emotions enter the game, all is lost. You don't make good decisions when you try to work on your emotions, but adding in those stop-losses will make sure that you use logic before the emotions have a chance to get in. If you wait until the trade has actually started, then you are already too late for the logic.

Chasing the Trends

Another area we need to be careful about as a beginner in day trading is chasing the trends. There are a lot of new traders who think it is best to wait for a bit of confirmation that they are right before they even think about entering their position. This hesitation may seem smart, but it causes them to miss some of the good entry points they want. And even if they are right, it could cause them to purchase a stock that has a price higher than they wanted.

Find a good strategy that you understand and trust, and wait for that to happen, but don't waste your time trying to follow the trend with all of this.

Not Waiting for Good Trades

As a new trader, you are probably really excited to get into the stock market and see what you can do. You want to show that you know what you are doing and that you can handle yourself, even in the fast-paced world of day trading. While it is great to have a lot of enthusiasm along the way, you do need to be careful here. If you jump in just because you are excited, you will definitely end up with a bad trade along the way.

As a new day trader, you need to have some patience ahead of time to make sure you get the right trade. And these good trades for day trading may not show up right away. You need to watch the charts and wait for some of the right signals that the technical analysis will show you. Experienced traders know that it is worth your time to wait for the right trade, rather than forcing the trade or entering it all at the wrong price and then they can overtrade their accounts.

Not Setting Your Own Rules and Sticking with Them

There is a lot that will change when you do begin trading. Sometimes the rules are easy to see and follow, and other times it may look like the market is all over the place. No matter what is going on with your trades or the market, you need to spend some time making rules you are comfortable with, and then sticking with them.

To make sure that you don't get yourself all caught up with your trades and all of the emotions that come with it (and letting emotions come into your trades can make it really hard to do well), of a big loss or a win, you need to establish some rules for each trade before it even starts. This means you need to have all of your entry and all of your exit points in place before you

211

enter the trade. And once they are in place, do not switch off them.

Professionals who spend a lot of time in the stock market, whether they work with day trading or another option, know that you can either focus on the trades, or you can think more about the rules. You can't spend your time doing both because you just can't concentrate on both. Staying objective and keeping those rules in mind from the start will help you to maintain all of the control you need with day trading.

Forgetting the Fundamentals Don't Matter

In many options out there for trading and investing, one of the techniques that you can use is the fundamental analysis. This is the technique that allows you to take a look at all the fundamentals that you need about the company and then use that to determine whether a particular stock is a good one to invest in. You would look at the management of the company, the customers they have, their potential to grow, and their finances. This is definitely a long-term strategy to work with, though, so won't have a lot of room inside the day traders plan.

New day traders will sometimes fall into the trap of looking at the company and assuming that for this kind of trading, if the company is good, it can never fail. Good companies fail on a regular basis, and since you are in the trade for such a short period of time, it really doesn't matter how good the company does. You just need them to perform well for the next few hours, and after that, they don't need to do all that well. There really isn't a lot of room for those fundamentals with day trading.

Traders who have spent some time working with day trading know how good the fundamentals of a company are will not really matter because they won't be in the market long enough for this to really show up. They instead choose to look at how the market is doing and how it is likely to behave for the next few hours or less.

The professional investor knows that when the market is currently selling down, even the prices of stock from a good company will go down. It is important to throw out the fundamentals and instead follow the signs of the market, and not really worry about anything else. This is a good technique for those who are working with long-term investments, but it is not a good idea for day traders who are not in the market all that long.

CHAPTER 31:

Some of the Top Traders in Stock Market

Warren Buffet

When it comes to giving financial advice, few people are able to captivate an audience quite like Warren Buffet can. His extraordinary success in the world of investments–not to mention his $85 billion fortune–means even those, not the slightest bit interested in finance sit up and listen when Buffett shares his top tips for amassing wealth.

Yet Buffett is more than just the sum of his bank balance (a ten-figure number to be exact). His life is shrouded in a passion for business and investments and, despite his vast wealth, he is widely known for his generosity and frugality–he still lives in the same home in Omaha in Nebraska that he bought for $31,000 in 1958 and more recently he has pledged to give away 99% of his wealth to charities.

His story is an intriguing one, to say the least. Who is Warren Buffet? What are some of his principles that you can apply in your life and business? What can you learn from Buffett's own experiences about managing your life, money and career?

Buffett has already confronted and overcome life's challenges and created a path that could serve as a winning roadmap for you. All you need to do is be willing to follow that path on your way to success. You'll need to tweak and customize it a little to meet your own situations and circumstances, but the blueprint is largely in place. In life and business, you can make the most of the wisdom learned by successful and wealthy people who've made a mark for themselves globally and use it as a guide to achieve your own goals.

For decades, Buffett has been a role model to thousands, if not millions, of budding entrepreneurs and people keen to make a difference in their lives. His success has influenced the actions of business people all around the world and has served as an exceptional standard to strive for both professionally and personally, thanks to his generosity and willingness to help others. His influence spreads far and wide and even those among the richest in the world have adopted Buffett's life approaches. Thanks to Buffett's encouragement, for example, more than 160 billionaires have agreed to donate and give away at least half of their wealth for philanthropic causes.

Paul Tudor Jones

Paul Tudor Jones is an American Investor, a hedge fund manager and he is also known as a philanthropist. Jones was born on September 28th, 1954. His love for Hedge fund management led him to open his firm back in 1980, a company by the name Tudor Investment Corporation. The company's headquarters were and are still based in Greenwich, connect cut, and it specialized in the management of assets. Later on, he created Tudor group, which is a hedge Fund Holding Company. The Tudor hedge company specialized in the management of fixed income, currencies, equities and also commodities.

Over the last years, his companies have been doing great earning him great fortunes since in February 2017, he was estimated to have a net of 4.7 billion by Forbes magazine and this made him be number 120 the of the wealthiest people in the world on the category of 400 people ranked on the magazine. Aside from this, Tudor 11 was also named as the 22nd highest and best-earning hedge manager worldwide. Aside from focusing on his hedge business, Tudor has also not been left behind when it comes to the love of humanity. This is traced back to the case where he opened the Robin food foundation just eight years after beginning his hedge firm. This foundation is solely focused on helping to eradicate poverty.

He was born in Memphis, and most of his life was spent there during school time. This is because he attended the Presbyterian day school and later joined all-boys elementary school, and also, he entered the Memphis high school. After graduating from high school, Jones then joined Virginia University, and he graduated with an undergraduate degree in economics in 1976.

He started to work immediately after he finished his college education because, in the same year that he graduated, he was able to secure employment at trading floors where he worked as the clerk. He worked there for four years, and in 1980, he was employed as the broker in E.F Hutton and companies. He worked in his new company for about two years before quitting claiming that he got bored by his job. Jones decided to further his education, and he applied at Harvard University in the business school category, although he did not attend the school.

Jones Tudor was first helped by his cousin who is the EO of Dunavant Enterprises a firm that is known to be among the top cotton merchants worldwide. William Dunavant introduced Tudor to a commodity broker by the name Eli Tullis who hired Jones in his cotton firm and still mentored him as well. He was trained on the trading and the brokerage work of the New York stock exchange.

According to Jones, Eli was the toughest and the best trainer he has ever come across as he taught him all the traits that one needs to become a successful businessman. He showed him how to withstand high competition in the markets, and he also warned him that whenever you have a business, you will always experience ups and downs in the line of your work.

Tim Cook

Timothy Donald Cook is the American executive, Industrial Engineer, and Developer. He is currently the Chief executive officer at the offices of Apple Inc. This is the new position he acquired at the Apple Inc. since he worked as the Chief Operating Officer under the founder Steve Jobs. Joined Apple in the year 1998 as the senior vice president of worldwide operations and then he later served as the executive vice president of the world in the department of sales and services. In 24th March 2011, he was promoted to become the Chief executive. He is remembered for his active advocation of various humanity and environmental growth, which include the reformation of political of international and local surveillance, cybersecurity, corporation taxation both nationally and internationally environments preservation and also the American manufacturing act.

In the year 2014, Cook became public and identified himself as gay and was listed among the 500 CEO at Fortune magazine. Other companies that Cook worked at include; he was a member of the board of boards of directors of Nike-Inc., the national football foundation, the trustee of Duke University.

Around 2012, the Apple Inc. company decided to give Cook a compensation of shares worth millions of dollars vesting in 2016 to 2021. During a public speech, Cook said that his earnings from the granted stocks would be offered to charity institutions. This includes all that he owns.

George Soros

George Soros was born in Budapest, Hungary, on August 12, 1930 as György Schwartz. He was born to Tivadar and Erzsébet Schwartz. The family was of Jewish descent but chose not to practice their religion due to the fact that anti-Semitism was on the rise in Hungary. As an upper-middle-class family, they did not wish to have their family to be under suspect and scrutinized. To avoid this, they changed their last name to Soros, which means "designated successor" in Hungarian. This name was liked by Soros' father not only for its meaning but also because it was spelled the same forward as it is backward.

After this name change, Nazi Germany came to occupy Hungary in March of 1944. The Nazis established a Jewish Council, Judunrat, in which all Jewish children had to report. They were no longer allowed to attend their regular schools. This council was in charge of deporting any Jews that were found in Hungary. They picked school-aged children to be the ones to bring the deportation notices to the people.

At this time, Soros was 13 years old and had received papers himself to give to Jewish lawyers. His father, Tivadar, advised him to warn the people as he handed them out that if they showed up to work that they would be deported.

During this precarious time, falsity needed to be made to protect many of the Jewish people. Soros' parents hid their Jewish roots yet again by purchasing documents that stated their "Christian" faith. This helped them survive through the Nazi occupation. Young George even had to pretend to be the "godson" to an official of the Hungarian government for his own protection. George was put in a situation where he had to go with this official to a Jewish family's estate to take inventory. He was not a part of the process himself, but had to witness the event. The official who was protecting Soros had his close connection to the Jewish people because his wife was Jewish as well. She had already gone into hiding at this point.

Through efforts like these, many Jewish people were protected in Hungary. The efforts of Soros's father to help people during this time solidified in young Soros's mind that his father was a great hero and a protector to the Jewish people.

Finally, an end came to the hiding in 1945 when the Nazi's left their occupation of Hungary. Soros was able to leave Hungary shortly after the Nazi receded in the year of 1947. Now he could pursue an education in London. He immigrated to England, where he attended the London School of Economics as a student of Carl Popper, a philosopher. In 1951, he received his Bachelor of Science in Philosophy. He ended school in 1954 with a Master of Science in philosophy.

CHAPTER 32:

Dos and Don'ts of Stock Market

Here are some of the dos and don'ts of stock markets that you have to bear in mind while making your investments.

Do's of Stock Market Trading

"Do" Your Research

The first thing is to do ample research on the subject. You have to know what some of the terms stand for and also what you have to do to make successful investments. You must read up online and gather more information. You can also turn to other good publications. There is nothing like enough information, and the more you read, the better. You will also have to buy yourself a basic guide that will teach you to operate the software that you will be using to buy and sell stocks.

You will need to research everything from available broker firms to country economies to current news and electronic trading options. Being well versed in the technology aspect of trading will be a big help to you.

Most brokers have their own proprietary trading software, which means that each software for each broker will differ slightly. Exchanges generally also develop their own software, often called matching engines, so if you are trading on different exchanges, you will also see slight differences there. Make sure that you are well versed in the differences so you do not make mistakes when going from one exchange to another.

When accessing the exchanges electronically, there are generally two different systems available to you—the GUI (graphical user interface) and the API (application programming interface). The GUI is an interface that is provided by the exchange and can be downloaded to your computer and the API is your own interface that will communicate with the exchange software. Your own API can be helpful if you are dealing with multiple exchanges and brokers, as it can display all of the information in one centralized place. APIs are often available for purchase from third parties. Unless you are well versed in software development, it is best to purchase an already functioning system, or use the system provided by your broker.

"Do" a Journal

Before you get started with your stock market investments, you have to research and find stocks that you think will do well. Look for those that will prove to be lucrative investments in the long run. If you wish to day trade, then you can look for penny stocks as they will rise and fall, in value, within a short period of time. You must always maintain a journal that will help you record your day-to-day stock market transactions. You can do this in writing, but an electronic journal is preferable as it can be easily searched for certain stocks or values.

It is also helpful if you keep your research journal separate from your purchase and sale journal. One should be used to track stocks you are interested in, even if you don't own them and the other used to write down all the investment transactions you are making, regardless of the instrument, or whether you are buying or selling.

It is easy to get carried away and many people make the mistake of not keeping track of how much they are spending and where, so a trading ledger will be just as important as a journal. Once again, an electronic ledger is the best option, as it can easily give you the most up to date information without having to do calculations after every single purchase or sale.

It is important to also have a plan in place which will prevent you from over-spending. It is a good idea to make a monthly budget for the investments that you will be making in a month and follow it to ensure that you spend wisely. The best budgeting method will be to divide your money up by investment category—a certain amount for stocks, for mutual funds, for precious metals, etc. This ensures that your portfolio remains diversified and that you don't spend all your money in one place and then end up losing your entire investment for the month. An electronic ledger will be the best option for your budget calculations as well.

"Do" a Risk Capital

Risk capital refers to money that you are willing to risk. It is capital that you should personally own and must not belong to someone else. Risk capital is also important for those that like taking risks in the market, like investing in penny stocks. Remember that the rule for day trading is that you must have 25% of your investments backed up by risk capital. It is best to keep your risk capital in a separate bank account from your other funds. This will keep you from overstepping your budget and completely depleting your resources.

If you borrow the money from someone else and invest it in the market, it is not considered risk capital, because then you will not be confident about your investments and keep wondering if you made a mistake. Therefore, it is vital that you invest money that completely belongs to you and no one else. In most cases, it would also be wise to not invest for someone else as they might have different expectations than you do.

"Do" a Diversification of Your Portfolio

You have to have a little of this and that in it so that the risk is diversified. Some people don't realize that putting all their money into the same security will cause their risk to double or even triple, as one simple mistake can lead to the loss of your entire risk capital. Therefore, it is important to invest in stocks, precious metals, foreign exchange, commodities, etc.

At the same time, it is also important to diversify within each of these categories to further diversify the risk. For example, you have to invest in different stocks belonging to different categories such as the agricultural sector, technology sector and energy sector. The same can be done for commodities. An example of a well-diversified portfolio would be the investment in gold, a retail company, a clean energy production company, wheat, coffee and a foreign currency such as the Japanese Yen.

"Do" Take the Help of Experts

It is a good idea to take the help of an expert. Some people might not be able to invest in the stock market with ease. There will be doubts and insecurities that have to be busted in order to make successful investments. For that, you can take the help of experts that you have in your life. If you know someone who trades in the stock market, you may not even have to pay someone to receive advice—all you have to do is look them up and seek their advice. They will be able to assist you with your investments.

Look at how they are trading and the types of stocks that they are picking. They may even allow you to sit in with them on a day of trading. Make sure to take careful notes and answer as many of your questions as possible. Are they holding on to investments for a long time or short selling them? Which exchanges and trading platforms do they use? What is their daily or monthly budget? Do they have a set goal for the return on their investments? These are some of the questions that you should answer.

Don'ts of Stock Market Trading

Here is the different don'ts that you have to bear in mind while making stock market investments.

Don't Copy Another

While taking advice from someone else is great for gaining more head knowledge, don't copy another person's investment plans as they will differ for each individual. You have to make an individualistic plan for yourself and not merely copy what is working for another person. Even if they are experiencing great success, you have to stick with whatever best suits your investment type.

Remember that each trade and sale have an impact on the market. Even though initially your investing will seem small, it still has an impact. You can look at the pattern used by other people and draw inspiration if you like, but it is best not to copy what they are doing as it might not work for you the same way. You can get them to advise you and come up with an investment plan if you like their choices. It's never a bad idea to run your investment ideas by an expert.

Don't Rush into Anything

Never rush into a decision, as you will end up making a mistake. Take your time with anything and everything, especially if you wish to remain invested for a long time. Be 100% sure about something in order to reap its full benefits. Wait and watch a stock for at least a month before deciding to invest in it. If you are happy with its performance, then invest in it.

This is especially hard to do if you are interested in day trading. The best advice would be to gain some experience in long-term investments first and then keep working downward with your time limit. Even day traders spend hours of time investigating and researching certain stocks that they may end up only owning for a minute or two, but every one of them will tell you that it is well worth the while.

Don't Ignore News

Don't ignore news about stocks. You have to go through the newspapers on a daily basis in order to know which stocks are good to invest in and which need to be avoided. You have to assess the market mood by studying the trends. Many people underestimate the value of reading through the suggested stock columns, thinking that it will not work for the masses but it will if you make the right moves.

Never make an investment without at least first reading the day's headlines. This may seem very tedious, but once it becomes a habit, you will find it quite enjoyable. Your knowledge base will begin to grow and compound, making it much easier to trade. Remember that investing is not like riding a bike, where you may not have been on a bike for years and then one day get on it and ride it like you never stopped. No, investment knowledge must be maintained. If you step out of day-to-day investing for a year or two, you will need to rebuild your entire knowledge base.

Don't Blindly Trust Message Boards

It is not advisable for you to blindly trust message boards, as there might be some bad advice present there. You have to do your own research in order to pick the best stocks for yourself. If you end up trusting another person's suggestions and buy bad stocks, then you will start hating the stock market. So be careful when you pick your stocks based on what the message boards have to say about them. Take everything with a grain of salt. Once you have begun investing, you will learn that your best advisor is your own gut and intuition that is fueled by knowledge.

Conclusion

Stock market investment is one of the best ways to protect your hard-earned money. During recession, most of the companies struggled to keep their heads above water, and the majority of the regular citizens started to protect their savings from irreparable loss. Most of the regular stock buyers started to walk away from the share markets, but few people who are intelligent purchased the shares which were at an unbelievable lower price. When the stock value of big companies fall you can purchase the stock at a lower price, and it is the best time to buy shares.

Stock market investment is no more a mystery, thanks to the era of the internet which helps you to set up your account from home and start a modern way of investing in the stock market. In the past, people have to run after the share brokers to know about the value of shares and to have a look at their account details. But these days everything has become transparent, and you can have a view at your account details and the recent prices of the stocks from being at home comfortably.

Well, only one thing is certain, and that is change. Changes are always certain, so does the experienced stock world. It has moved on to cyberspace from the clattered, clumsy stock markets, which looks nonetheless fish markets. The evolution of the Internet is the reason for the revolution in stock markets as well as another trading. It got the easy access feature along with the comfort of operating stocks from one's office or home. The speedy technology acted as a catalyst to break the norms of the stock market. It is no more an alien world for people. Rather, it got unearthed, and the mysteriousness of this trading place just vanished. Now, people are comfortable trading online, and the investors and their investments have increased three-fold. The bulls and bears are no more only confined to the creams rather it has skimmed to the commons.

Being a stock-market investor, you should keep an eye on the market trend and ready to face the downfall at any time as there are risks in this business that are fairly high and severe in some cases.

You should know about the company and the market trends before investing your precious money in the stock market. The company's future goals and aspirations can be very helpful for you to make the right decisions.

At the end of a well-run marathon, fatigue is accompanied by an exhilarating sense of achievement. All the planning, all the obsessing, all the training in all types of weather: it all seems worth it. Not just "worth it," but an invaluable experience that, I believe, makes one a better person.

With a well-run investment plan, you get the same sense of accomplishment. Long-range planning and patience pay off. College education for your children and a comfortable retirement for you: you have set your goals and achieved them. And, if you invest successfully enough, you may choose to donate some of your profits to charities and causes you support—making you a better person and the world a better place.

Just as importantly, you will be in control of your finances. You will become comfortable with the ups and downs of the market and of individual stocks. You will hold high-quality dividend-paying stocks for the long term. You will know what could go wrong, but you will also know there is a lot that can (and probably will) go right.

Perhaps you never thought you could do it. Now you know you can, so why not give it a shot?

9 781802 679411